WALKING WITH YOUR SPIRIT TOTEM ANIMALS

ALSO BY SHAWN LEONARD

Spirit Talker: Indigenous Stories and Teachings from a Mikmaq Psychic Medium

Wisdom of the Elders Oracle: A 44-Card Deck and Guidebook

All of the above are available at your local bookstore, or may be ordered by visiting:

Hay House UK: www.hayhouse.co.uk
Hay House USA: www.hayhouse.com®
Hay House Australia: www.hayhouse.com.au
Hay House India: www.hayhouse.co.in

WALKING WITH YOUR SPIRIT TOTEM ANIMALS

Discovering the Four Animals That Guide You Through Life

SHAWN LEONARD

HAY HOUSE

Carlsbad, California • New York City
London • Sydney • New Delhi

Published in the United Kingdom by:
Hay House UK Ltd, 1st Floor, Crawford Corner,
91–93 Baker Street, London W1U 6QQ
Tel: +44 (0)20 3927 7290; www.hayhouse.co.uk

Text © Shawn Leonard, 2025

Cover design: Jordan Wannemacher • Interior design: Bryn Starr Best
Interior illustrations pages 72, 73: Shawn Leonard
Interior illustrations pages 92, 102, 108, 115, 124, 130, 136, 144, 153: Courtesy of Shutterstock

All rights reserved. No part of this book may be reproduced by any mechanical, photographic or electronic process, or in the form of a phonographic recording; nor may it be stored in a retrieval system, transmitted or otherwise be copied for public or private use, other than for 'fair use' as brief quotations embodied in articles and reviews, without prior written permission of the publisher.

The information given in this book should not be treated as a substitute for professional medical advice; always consult a medical practitioner. Any use of information in this book is at the reader's discretion and risk. Neither the author nor the publisher can be held responsible for any loss, claim or damage arising out of the use, or misuse, of the suggestions made, the failure to take medical advice or for any material on third-party websites.

A catalogue record for this book is available from the British Library.

Tradepaper ISBN: 978-1-83782-487-8
E-book ISBN: 978-1-4019-9726-7
Audiobook ISBN: 978-1-4019-9688-8

10 9 8 7 6 5 4 3 2 1

This product uses responsibly sourced papers, including recycled materials and materials from other controlled sources. For more information, see www.hayhouse.co.uk

The authorized representative in the EU for product safety and compliance is Penguin Random House Ireland, Morrison Chambers, 32 Nassau Street, Dublin D02 YH68, Ireland. https://eu-contact.penguin.ie

Printed and bound by CPI Group (UK) Ltd, Croydon CR0 4YY

♦ ♦ ♦ ♦

This book is dedicated to all my relations, including my Animal Totems, who have walked with me through life even when, in my youth, I was not aware of their existence or significance to me, spiritually and culturally. They have provided me with bravery, wisdom, strength, and spiritual insight throughout all the different stages of my life.

Thank you to all the Elders who have taught me about who I really am as an Indigenous person. Thank you to the many generous donors of Animal Medicines that I work with and that I hold dear as I move forward in life as White Eagle Spirit Talker.

Thank you for the contributions of my Spirit Talker Tribe, who also live and work with their Animal Totems and their medicines and have shared their stories with me. Lastly, I wish that all people, from all walks of life, learn to discover who walks beside them in the spirit world, the Spirit Totem Animals who are sending them Animal Medicine and guiding them in life so they can live their life in a good way.

*Wela'lioq—Msit No'kmaq.
Thank you—All my relations.*

♦ ♦ ♦ ♦

CONTENTS

◆ ◆ ◆ ◆

Foreword ix
Introduction xi

CHAPTER 1: What Is a Totem? 1

CHAPTER 2: My Father, the Skunk, and What the Rabbit Taught Me .. 5

CHAPTER 3: I Come to You for Help 11

CHAPTER 4: As Long as We're Together, We're Family...............17

CHAPTER 5: Animal Family, Spirit Connections 23

CHAPTER 6: Indigenous People and Their Connection to the Animal Nation............................... 31

CHAPTER 7: Discovering the Medicine of the White Buffalo 39

CHAPTER 8: Finding an Elder 45

CHAPTER 9: Totems Reveal Themselves 51

CHAPTER 10: Spirit Talker and the White Buffalo 59

CHAPTER 11: The Owl—My Final Totem Reveals Itself 65

CHAPTER 12: The Four Animal Medicines That Walk with Us in Life 71

CHAPTER 13: Sacred Animals Around the World 77

CHAPTER 14: Identifying and Working with Our Animal Totems 85

The Importance of the Seven Grandfather Teachings 96

CHAPTER 15: Humility—The Wolf 97

CHAPTER 16: Truth—The Turtle 103

CHAPTER 17: Bravery—The Bear 109

CHAPTER 18: Love—The Eagle 117

CHAPTER 19: Respect—The Bison or Buffalo 125

CHAPTER 20: Wisdom—The Beaver 131

CHAPTER 21: Honesty—Sabe or Bigfoot 137

CHAPTER 22: The Moose Harvest 145

CHAPTER 23: There Is Always Hope at Hope for Wildlife 155

CHAPTER 24: Animal Messengers and Forerunners 161

CHAPTER 25: White Buffalo Calf Woman and Prophecy 169

CHAPTER 26: Walking with Your Totems 179

Acknowledgments 185
About the Author 187

FOREWORD

♦ ♦ ♦ ♦

Last year I had the gift of meeting Shawn, White Eagle Spirit Talker—Wape'k Kitpu Aknutmajik Jijaqmij—in person. In sharing meals and relating in a good way, I discovered that Shawn is an incredible storyteller—his medicine makes my Indigenous heart feel right at home.

I could relate deeply to Shawn's stories of walking between two worlds and his ability to hear the spirit world so clearly. And in reading *Walking with Your Spirit Totem Animals*, I can further relate to the continuous reclamation and remembering journey that we are on as Indigenous people.

Shawn's stories about the medicine that the animal realm carries invite us to think beyond our tendency to see our journey as individualistic. The words of this book constantly bring us back to the truth that we are all connected, not just with one another but with all creation. The word *Indinawemaaganidog* in Ojibway means "all my relatives," and in the stories shared here, we learn that our animal friends are indeed allies, kin, and family. Therefore, all our words, intentions, and choices impact them, now and in the seven generations to come.

Animal Spirits have been some of my greatest teachers, guardians and protectors, and much like Shawn, they have shown up over and over again as messengers. I love the teaching shared in this book that we all walk with four animals as I, too, have found this to be true. Deer teaches compassion to me on my lupus journey, Bear reminds me to set boundaries and rest, Eagle helps me share my vision with the world, and Thunderbird helps me to be the trailblazer. This book allows you to reflect on which Spirit Totem Animal may be moving with you through your life and provides you with the knowing that you are never alone on this journey.

The Seven Grandfather Teachings that are shared in *Walking with Your Spirit Totem Animals* are teachings that everyone should know and learn about. If we all moved on the Earth Mother with them, the world would be in a much better place. In meeting Shawn, I can confirm that he embodies the teachings powerfully. Walking closely with this wisdom involves a different level of consciousness than what we are currently experiencing on the Earth at this time, and this book gives me hope that change is coming.

I offer a prayer for our world:

May we all walk with love,
tending to the fractures of our hearts
so that more light can pass through.

May we all walk with humility,
remembering that we are one with creation.

May we all walk with bravery,
standing for the Earth and all her inhabitants.

May we all walk with respect,
holding another as sacred.

May we all walk with truth,
coming home to integrity within ourselves.

May we all walk with honesty,
returning to alignment in mind, body, and spirit.

May we all walk with wisdom,
calling forth on the ancestors that live in our bones and blood.

May this book invoke your connection to the Spirit Totem Animals in a way that serves and supports you so that you can rise into the medicine you were meant to be. I am eternally grateful that Shawn has risen into his, and I am proud to call him my niijii (friend).

Asha Frost,
Nenaandawi Nagweyaab Kwe—Healing Rainbow Woman

INTRODUCTION

♦ ♦ ♦ ♦

Have you ever wondered why you feel drawn to a particular animal as opposed to another? Have you felt more connected to one animal at a particular stage in your life, whether in your Youth, in Adulthood, or in your Elder stage of life? Have you felt drawn to specific animals at different times along your life's journey and you didn't know why?

Throughout this book, I will take you on my own sacred journey of understanding how the Animal Nation has been connected to me.

My life has been completely transformed since I embraced my Indigenous culture and incorporated the Animal Medicines that came to me at different stages of life. Part of who I am is deeply connected to my Mi'kmaq name: Wape'k Kitpu Aknutmajik Jijaqmij, which literally means White Eagle Spirit Talker. There is a clear connection between White Eagle Medicine that comes from the sacred Eagle and my own spirit. I'm sure that whether you have an Indigenous name or not, if you were to be given one, it would also deeply connect to a Spirit Animal of yours.

Even without having a name ceremony done and an Indigenous name bestowed upon you, you may already know which animals connect with you strongly. Dr. Wayne Dyer, a spiritual teacher who has influenced me throughout my life, said, "If you knew who walked beside you at all times . . . you could never experience fear or doubt again." Connecting to my own Power Totems and Spirit Totems has helped me along my life's journey, and I hope you will connect with yours as well.

WALKING WITH YOUR SPIRIT TOTEM ANIMALS

Within the book there are many personal experiences and teachings, including a ceremonial meditation, a sacred prayer, and a questionnaire for you to connect to your Spirit Totem Animals and the specific medicines that they bring to you in your life journey.

I also describe the Seven Grandfather Teachings, which focus on animals such as the Wolf, Turtle, Bear, Eagle, Bison and Buffalo, Beaver, and Sabe or Bigfoot. There are also sacred prayers to work with the medicines of each of these animals. I know these Animal Medicines will help you walk through life in the best way possible for you.

> Wela'lin—Msit No'kmaq.
> Thank you—All my relations.
>
> Wape'k Kitpu Aknutmajik Jijaqmij
> White Eagle Spirit Talker
>
> **Shawn Leonard**

CHAPTER 1

♦ ♦ ♦ ♦

Wen N+t To'tm?

WHAT IS A TOTEM?

When I was young, I thought of totem poles when I heard the word *totem*. In Mi'kmaq culture in the eastern part of Canada, making totem poles was never part of our culture; it wasn't a profound belief. Totem poles are more of a Pacific West Coast tradition, as I've seen in British Columbia while filming my show *Spirit Talker*. While totem poles might not specifically represent one's Totem Animals, there may be one on a pole that a person is deeply connected to. The other animals on the pole may just tell a story about something that was going on at some time in the past.

What I've learned from talking to different carvers in Western Canada is that there are three different kinds of poles: welcoming poles, house poles, and totem poles. The difference between a totem and a house pole is that a totem pole is usually out in a public place to welcome visitors with outstretched wings or arms at the top, while a house pole can have representations of a clan and also a general story of the animals that are carved on them.

Welcoming poles may have an animal carved on them, and they are put in locations where visitors will see them when they arrive at a place where they know they are welcomed. Usually a figure of a community or tribe will be featured at the top of the welcoming pole with arms or wings outstretched to welcome people coming to the community. The message to visitors is profound: "We embrace you."

It wasn't until I visited some communities in British Columbia while filming *Spirit Talker* that I understood more fully what totem poles actually are. I was in Cowichan Tribes First Nation Community, the largest Indigenous community in British Columbia, when I met a carver named Herb Rice. He was currently commissioned to do an art piece to commemorate people who died of asbestos poisoning in the last century. A project like that could take him six months from start to finish, he told me. He calls his totems Salish Story Totems, and he makes them for the Pacific Northwest. Herb showed me the hand tools that he had made and sharpened himself to carve the poles. He very kindly allowed me to give carving a try.

Herb believes that a totem pole starts with a deep energy, and as I placed my hands on the totem pole he was working on, I could feel the energy of the totem. All things have a spirit or an aura, as I call it. That particular tree was estimated to be six or seven hundred years old, a red cedar old-growth tree. It is incredible to think that that cedar has seen many of our ancestors as they walked past it. I felt honored to touch its spirit.

When I went to British Columbia near Vancouver for Season 5, Episode 7 of *Spirit Talker*, I visited a very small community called Tsawwassen First Nation, where I met a well-known carver named Karl Morgan, who creates house poles and welcoming poles. As we went for a walk along the Salish Sea, he told me that he gets inspiration for his artwork by spending time walking there. Historically, Indigenous people would have stopped there while waiting for favorable tides before setting off toward the islands, so there would always have been welcoming poles there by the water. They are still there, with the wings of eagles and some with hands or arms opened wide, extended at the top of the poles in a gesture of welcoming, to welcome people to their shores. He told me it is important to remember that when we see a totem or a house pole, it is telling the story of the land. The cedars that are being carved are considered their ancestors and are regarded as gifts that tell a story.

The pole he was working on at the time told the legend of the Tsawwassen Nation and of Princess Tsawwassa. It told the story of how his ancestors came down from the mountain and settled on the beach to have a warmer climate and to be closer to all the abundant sea life, including salmon. Karl tries to create art that tells the legends as accurately as possible. Many of his poles can be seen around the community. He wants people to have pride in their heritage.

I got another chance during my visit to try my hand at carving a totem. I was honored to be a part of that creation. Carvers like Herb and Karl are carving a cultural legacy. None of us is going to live forever, so we need to pass down our sacred teachings from generation to generation so our culture can stay in the world.

But totems are also our Spirit Animals, and that is what I want to teach in this book. Animal Totems are sacred animals that walk with us in spirit throughout our lives. They are animalistic symbols that represent qualities that will help us. They offer us their Animal Medicines, which are not physical remedies but the animals' unique traits, energies, and lessons that help, guide, protect, and walk with us through our daily life. When I say totems, that's what I am referring to in this book.

Even though I know four of my totems, I could tell a story on a totem pole about the different phases of my life in which an animal presented itself to me. But as it's not part of my culture, I don't need to do that. What I am doing as a Mi'kmaq person is sharing my understanding of and teaching about what Spirit Totem Animals are for me, which Animal Medicines they bring to me, and how everyone can walk through life with their own Animal Totems to guide them with their particular medicines.

Whether we have read about the Seven Grandfather Teachings yet or not, it will become evident that animals have specific qualities or medicines that we can incorporate into our being and our engagement with life, and they can be called upon at different times to move us through the world in a good way. Even though we may know our totems, we may still need to call upon the medicines of other animals as we face different challenges. We may call upon the humility of the Wolf, the truth of the Turtle, the bravery of the Bear, the love of the Eagle, the respect of the Bison, the wisdom of the Beaver, or the honesty of Sabe at different points in our life. Even though we each carry our particular Totem Animal Medicines, we can also call upon other Animal Medicines to help us if we feel the need to.

Our own particular Spirit Animals walk with us throughout our lives. Let's continue, and learn together who helps, protects, lends wisdom, and brings peace and harmony between the Human Nation and the Animal Nation.

CHAPTER 2

♦ ♦ ♦ ♦

Nujj, Apukjilu, aq Ta'n Apli'kmuj Ekina'muij

MY FATHER, THE SKUNK, AND WHAT THE RABBIT TAUGHT ME

Growing up, my interaction and engagement with the Animal Nation was predominantly through my father. My father was Metis, and he taught me about the sacredness of the life of all the animals that we would hunt for food. He taught me to be grateful for the life force that I was taking from them for our sustenance. In spite of this, being in my early teens, I was very much detached, not thinking about the spirits of the animals. My dad taught me respect, and that if I were going to go out hunting, I should not go out just shooting anything. If I were going to take an animal's life, I had better eat it. In that way, I would honor the animal. As Indigenous people, we have to honor the sacredness of the animal and use every part of it, not deliberately wasting anything and taking only what we need.

My dad and I went out hunting every year. He was in the navy, but he was always home in the fall to go deer hunting. He was a phenomenal sharpshooter. He was probably the only man I ever knew who could shoot a dime from 200 yards away. Though he had impeccable marksmanship, he was not so lucky at hunting. I would go hunting with my dad, and we would not see one deer. It didn't matter what we did, where we went, there were no deer. It was just like we were never meant to. Unfortunately, my father died young, when he was 42, and I was only 15, so we never had the opportunity to see a deer together. I think it was the spirit world that prevented us from ever seeing one. In a way, I was grateful, because harvesting an animal is a lot of work, but on the other hand, I was kind of looking forward to learning about harvesting an animal and using all the things that an animal could give us; I was able to learn that much later in life.

My father did teach me other things, though, such as trapping and rabbit snaring. A rabbit snare is like a wire noose, and a rabbit that gets caught in one dies quickly of suffocation. When I was young, I didn't trap very much, but I became very good at rabbit snaring. I caught many rabbits over the years, and I have two stories that I want to tell in relation to that. For a young person growing up in Elmsdale, Nova Scotia, Canada, in the backwoods out in the middle of nowhere, there wasn't much around and there wasn't much work for a young person to do. I really didn't have any money or anything for myself, so I would often snare rabbits during the winter and sell them to my neighbors. That's how I would make some money: fifteen dollars for two rabbits. I'd catch up to 12 rabbits a week.

I would journey through the middle of the woods on my snowshoes and my skis, navigating the deep snow in the silence of the woods, hiking for miles and miles by myself. I would set my snares and then go back in a day or two to check on them. It was fairly cold in the winter back then—winters are much milder now than they were when I was young. My mother had bought me a very warm wool coat to make sure I kept warm while I was out in the woods. I would check my snares, which would have two or three rabbits that I would then bring home and clean. Some we would eat, and some we would sell because that was the only way I could make money. My dad taught me to honor the animals accordingly by showing me how to make gloves and mittens out of the pelts and to see if there was something else I could do with their fur. My dad taught me to do stuff like that because it is important in Indigenous culture not to waste anything that an animal can give us.

One time when I went out to check on one of my snares, it looked like I had gotten a rabbit. The animal was partly covered by a fresh snowfall, and as I was brushing the snow off what I thought was a rabbit, I suddenly realized the animal was still very much alive and that it was not a rabbit at all, but a skunk! The skunk sprayed me pretty good, and I didn't know what to do, because every time I would go near the skunk, it would spray. The stink that the skunk emitted was so strong, I could actually see the smell. If you've ever seen heat waves coming up from the hot pavement in the summertime, the air was like that. I had to go home to get my father. My new wool coat was so drenched with the stink of the skunk that my dad said the air around me was almost folding in on itself!

We went back to the snare together, and we struggled with the skunk. Of course, my dad made me do all the work because it was a lesson for me. We got a garbage bag, and I was able to put the garbage bag on the back end of the skunk even though it kept spraying. I held it down by the back of the neck, my dad was able to snip the snare off, and the skunk went away. I felt really bad about harming the skunk.

Another time, as I was going along on my journey of hunting, harvesting, and snaring animals, I caught a rabbit that was still alive. This experience changed my entire outlook on snaring. It was because I saw that the rabbit was still alive but that it wasn't going to survive for very long. I had to make a decision that I really didn't want to make. Unfortunately, it had a tear on its neck from the snare, and it cried. It was crying for its life. My dad told me that I had to honor the spirit of the animal and could not let an animal suffer. I knew the right thing to do would be to put the rabbit down, and I did, swiftly, with my gun. I brought the rabbit home, harvested it in the way that my father had taught me, and used the fur to make a mitten, then we ate the rabbit in a stew because I did not waste any of the animals that I caught.

After that day, I decided I didn't want to hunt anymore. I didn't want to hurt another animal ever again. I knew that the rabbit was teaching me something. When I had to look that rabbit in the eyes and end its life, I understood that it wanted to live just as much as I did. I understood that we've all been given a life, and that life is sacred. It also taught me about gratitude for all living things. Much later in life, I learned about an Indigenous teaching named Msit No'kmaq, which means "all my relations." It is one of the teachings that I live by, and you will see me mention it many times in this book. I learned this from many Elders, and I think that rabbit was teaching me back in the day that everything has a spirit.

We all have to nourish ourselves and find sustenance for our life, whether we are vegetarian, vegan, or neither. According to Indigenous people, all the plants that we take also have a spirit. The trees that we harvest to build our homes also have a spirit. The fields from which we take the wheat to make our bread also have a spirit. Indigenous people offer tobacco in a ceremony before taking in their crops. It was that rabbit, that day, that taught me about the sacredness of life and taught me to be grateful for all the food that I had eaten.

That's why I think that many different belief systems celebrate animals in different ways and for different reasons, especially when it comes to food and sustenance. There's gratitude and grace, and I was even taught that we should say grace before eating our food. There is a sacredness of life to it all, even the carrots that we pick out of our gardens. We are all related, and it's important that I share the teaching of what the rabbit taught me that day when I had to look it in the eyes and unfortunately end its life. The rabbit taught me about the sacredness of life and of being grateful for all the food that I have. We don't think about that when we buy our chicken, our beef, or even our rice that we boil for our food. It all has a life. We are all connected; everything has a spirit even though I know that many people think that in relation to animals, they are different. We also don't think about the spirit of the plants, and there's truth to this too.

There are studies in relation to plants that show that the intention we have, if we speak to our plants, the energy that we give our plants, affects them. There is an energy, a life force, that responds to the energy that we give them. So with all our food, including the Animal Nation, we should be grateful and honor the animals' flesh, honor the life they have given to provide us sustenance for life. I know the rabbit taught me that lesson that day, and I have never hunted again.

That doesn't mean I'm opposed to people who hunt, and I may hunt again in the future for a moose or some other wild game, but I would do a ceremony ahead of time. I would lay tobacco down. If I take the moose's life, if I choose to do that in the future, I know that I have to honor the animal and the life that it has given to provide me with sustenance.

Some people believe that if a person is very spiritually evolved, they should not eat animals anymore and should become vegan or vegetarian, but this is not what Indigenous people have been doing for centuries. We could not have survived on only blueberries and tea. Indigenous people see all things as having a spirit and a life force. Not eating animals is like saying that plant life is less sacred than animal life, but Indigenous wisdom teaches that all life forms are equally as sacred and we should be equally as grateful for the life force that we are taking from them for our sustenance. People plant flowers and love them, but they eat vegetables. Tell the air that it is more important than the water. Tell the bee that the flower is not special.

It's just a matter of perspective, how we look at things. One of my daughters, Sianna, has a great love and a deep compassion for animals that is even greater than mine. She chose to be vegan for many years. I respected her decision to become vegan, as it is a personal one, and we must all follow our own conscience. Now, however, she bounces back and forth between being vegan and vegetarian. She sometimes incorporates animal products into her life, like eggs and cheese, but will not eat meat.

Everything has a life force and an energy, and it's important to honor the life force and energy of all things and to respect the life they give us. We must express gratitude for all living things that sustain us. We honor all things by only taking what we need. We honor the animals by using every part of them, as much as we can. My father taught me to honor all animals, to respect them, and to be grateful for their life that we are taking for our sustenance, but I was not ready yet to receive this lesson, so Spirit sent me two animals to help me learn about the sacredness of life. I think the skunk was trying to teach me, but I did not understand, so Spirit sent me the rabbit to bring the lesson home, the lesson of Msit No'kmaq. All my relations.

CHAPTER 3

♦ ♦ ♦ ♦

Pekisinn Kwil+m Apoqnmasuti

I COME TO YOU FOR HELP

After my experiences with the skunk and the rabbit, I started to shift my whole perspective toward animals, realizing that they wanted to live, just as I wanted to live. I started to have a lot more empathy for the Animal Nation. The spirit world must have recognized that I had this empathy, because all of a sudden, animals were coming to me for help. They seemed to be drawn to me at that point. Dr. Wayne Dyer often referred to St. Francis of Assisi, who said of animals, "Not to hurt our humble brethren is our first duty to them, but to stop there is not enough. We have a higher mission: to be of service to them wherever they require it."

I felt this shift in my own energy once I had no wish to harm another animal and I stopped hunting. My compassion for all animals drew them to me for help.

Once, a crow came to me. I kept it for two weeks. I fed it and gave it water, although I didn't know what was wrong with the crow. It didn't look very well. It looked like it could potentially die, but after keeping it in a box in my garage for a while, it was able to get out of the box and get around the garage. I would leave it some cat food and some water, and it seemed to like that. Then, when I felt that the crow was strong enough, I opened the garage door and the crow was gone. I never saw it again.

What really struck me was that after I had let the crow go, many crows came around the house. I wonder if that injured crow was being watched the whole time by its family. Maybe it told the other crows that my house was a good place to hang out! I do know that crows remember people. The more I observed them, the more I started to realize that they could talk to each other, and I think I even figured out what some of their language meant.

I noticed that they would always call out to each other. It would be a very basic conversation of sorts. I remember that one crow seemed to be the oldest crow, or there would be a crow couple and there would be a bunch of other crows in their little family, called a murder of crows, but I don't really like that term. One crow would always sound off to the other crows. They would call once, and another crow would answer once from a different place. Then the crow would call three times, then another crow in the distance would call back three times. Sometimes a crow would call two times, and another crow would answer two times. It seemed like they were telling each other where they were in relation to each other. I eventually figured out that they were always checking on each other to see where they were, keeping track of the family members. They would spread out, and then when there was food, they would all gather.

I even started to feed the crows bread and table scraps out in my yard. They weren't too keen on me watching them eat, so I would peek out the window to see them. As a young boy, I was always interested in what they were doing. Eventually, they seemed to come around me more because they knew that I would give them food.

Next, I came across a raccoon that had a bad paw. It had gotten hit by a car and seemed to be immobile. So I brought the raccoon home, put it in a crate in my garage, fed it, and gave it water. We named him Coonie. About three or four weeks later, I opened up the garage door and let the raccoon, now healthy, go back into nature.

My mom jokingly blames me because now she has a generational raccoon problem. She has a garden, and they all come for the feast in her yard. They mostly eat the wine grapes, but also the apples and the pears. One year, she captured 27 raccoons and dropped them off far away at the airport to relocate them. She says it is my fault, because ever since I rescued and fed that one raccoon long ago, it told its raccoon friends and they all just kept coming every year, just like the crows had done. Whenever my mom would go away to Newfoundland, and even to this day, if she is late coming back by a week or so, there won't be one grape left.

After that I rescued various birds that had hit a window and needed help. I would pick them up and put them in a box because they seemed kind of stunned, just to give them a safe space to get well; a bird laying on the ground would not be safe. We always had a cat, and I didn't want any cat of mine to kill a bird that had been injured, so I would keep the bird in a box in the garage to make sure that my cat couldn't get in there. Once I saw that the bird was looking spry and flying around the garage, I would make sure my cat was indoors and leave the garage door open to let the bird fly back out.

We would adopt stray cats. We had the Disney book *The Aristocats*, and we would name all our cats after those characters in the book, like Charlie, Burly, Duchess, and Tom. My mom actually kept one of the strays and called her Rascal. That cat showed up at our house with a limp, like it had something wrong with its paw. It had gotten injured somehow. Rascal was a striped tabby with a little bit of white fur, and she was a bit overweight too. She was an amazing cat and was a great help to my mom after my dad passed. For some reason, she came to our house seeking help, and she just never went away!

I knew that it was because of my shifting energy toward the Animal Nation that all these wild animals and strays would be drawn to our home. My energy changed from indifference toward an animal's emotions and feelings, their life force and energy, to one of compassion. When I began rescuing and caring for injured animals, I started to have more compassion for them. When I saw them differently from the way I had been seeing them as a hunter, my relationships with the animals changed. They started to come to me for help. It allowed me to nurture relationships with different animals, like the crow, the raccoon, the stray cat, and various birds that I would care for and nurse back to health. I became like an animal doctor all of a sudden, like Dr. Dolittle. I felt like all these animals were starting to come to me instead of running from me because I was no longer trying to trap them. It was really about how I felt about them, so anything I could do for an animal that was injured or harmed, I would do. I kind of felt like I was working out my karma that I had taken on because of the harm I had done to so many animals. Even though I knew that we needed animals for sustenance, there are other ways to get sustenance than hunting them myself. Although it's a very Indigenous aspect to honor the animals and their lives, I had a shift in consciousness surrounding the Animal Nation.

The Creator, my guides, my ancestors knew that I had learned that lesson, so they were sending me animals to connect to in a much different way as opposed to using them for food or to make money. I moved away from eating animals that I would trap. I moved away from doing the hunting myself. I just honored the animals that would come to me that needed my help. When we shift our energy toward the Animal Nation, they will come to us, they will seek help from us.

I felt inspired by St. Francis of Assisi, who is said to have drawn animals to him. "For it is in giving that we receive," said St. Francis. The more I gave to the Animal Nation that came to me for help, the more animals I received. When animals do need help, they will seek out people who can help them. When I was in alignment with helping and serving, the animals seemed to know this.

To this day, crows are still drawn to me. I live close to a wildlife rescue called Hope for Wildlife here in Nova Scotia. A few years ago, I was working outside at my house with my friend Grant when a crow came up to my doorstep. It could walk, but it seemed like it couldn't fly, and it also seemed a little out of it. It walked right up to my front doorstep and up to my shoe. It just stood there looking at me. I noticed it had a silver tag on its ankle. I brought it some food and water, but it wouldn't eat. It just stayed there looking at me.

I went inside and called Hope for Wildlife and asked if they were missing a crow. They replied, "Funny you should ask that, because we are!" When I got off the phone with them and went back outside, the crow was gone. All of Hope for Wildlife came to my house and were looking for it around the house, in the trees, the woods, everywhere, but the crow was nowhere to be found. Apparently it *could* fly. What I found odd was that it came to me, of all people. Why? Why wasn't it scared of me? I do feed the crows all the time, but this crow seemed to come up to me and tell me that it needed help.

I went down to Hope for Wildlife later on, and there was a crow there that was caged because it could not fly. It was a female crow named Tilly. When she saw me, she almost purred for me. The volunteers told me she only liked men, especially bearded men. I didn't have a beard, but when I put my hand into her crate, she walked over to me and bowed down to let me pet her head. It would have been cool if

Tilly had been the crow that came to visit me that day, but she wasn't.

Did the crow that came to me and sat on my shoe communicate with the other wild crows that I feed daily that I was to be trusted? I wonder about things like that. I don't know if the crow that visited me on my doorstep went back to Hope for Wildlife or not. I do know that it came to me, stared at me, stood on my shoe, and then flew away before it could be caught again! It knew, somehow, that I was a person it could trust and I wasn't going to harm it.

If we are spiritually in tune with the Animal Nation, animals will come to us and communicate their needs to us. Once my energy shifted toward the Animal Nation, I experienced a real gift and a blessing to have all those animals come to me for help. They started to embrace me instead of fearing me.

There is a fox den near my house, and I often see them out, lounging about, the kits and the adult foxes too, and I talk to them and tell them not to sleep on the road because it's dangerous. They look at me as I talk to them, and they seem to be listening to me. I want to make sure that they are safe, and I feel that I have a duty of care to all animals in the Animal Nation, as St. Francis would encourage us to have.

CHAPTER 4

♦ ♦ ♦ ♦

Teli Piji Toqeyi'k, Kinu Jiksu'k

AS LONG AS WE'RE TOGETHER, WE'RE FAMILY

As I continued to shift my energy from hunter to rescuer, my compassion for the Animal Nation grew to the point of seeing animals as companions and members of my family as well, even to the present day. The Animal Nation was deeply connected to my personal life moving forward. The list of cats with *Aristocats* names that we rescued or took in grew longer as the years passed. Then, eventually, at a time when our family really needed her, a dog came into our life. For the rest of my life there would always be a member of the Animal Nation blended into my life as a true member of my family.

One of the cats we rescued stands out in my mind. His name was Charlie. He was a massive orange and white long-haired cat. He was truly a companion, a member of our family. Charlie would follow us around wherever we went, just like a dog. When we went blueberry picking up the hill, he would follow us up the hill and lay there as we collected berries, and then he would follow us back home afterward.

He would follow us down the hill to the school bus and wait at the bus stop with us in the morning, and he would be there waiting for us on the hill to walk home with us when the bus dropped us off at the end of the school day. Even though he belonged to the Animal Nation, he was truly a member of our human family.

After my father passed away, we adopted a dog named Weasley. She was an Old English Sheepdog and terrier mix, twice the size of her little terrier mother. She was black and white with short, curly fur. My brother went to school with someone whose family was giving puppies away, and he was the one who chose Weasley. Once he brought the puppy home, even though he really wanted the dog, she just became my dog instead. We had a special bond.

When we first got her, she was whining so much that we put her downstairs in the furnace room at night. She would sleep down in the basement in a box, and I would go down there with my pillow and a blanket and sleep on the floor with her to keep her company. She saw me as her protector. She was very intelligent, and I taught her a lot of tricks. My neighbor Wade would come over, and even though she loved him, every time I would ask her, "What do you think of Wade?" she would make a low, growling noise! She did that with everybody. It didn't matter who. She was very protective of me.

Weasley hung out with me all the time and followed me pretty much everywhere I went. She loved going out in the woods with me when I went hiking, swimming, fishing, or camping. I would always bring her with me in the backwoods. She was my companion, my friend, and my protector. Once she chased a bear out of the woods that I didn't even know was there while I was going fishing and swimming. It was an adolescent black bear, not fully grown yet. It was eating blueberries, and Weasley scared it away.

I left home when Weasley was only five, so she became my mother's dog at that point. My mom spoiled her with all kinds of foods a dog shouldn't eat, but Weasley was a good companion for her. My mother was still grieving for my father at that point, following his death, and having an animal to care for took her mind off her sorrow to some degree. Weasley was good for my mom. She was really a true member of our family. Weasley helped my mother to heal.

When I got older and was living in Calgary, I had an incredible bond with a cat named Stormy. I adopted her when I met the mother of my children. She was a brown-and-black brindled cat with one orange patch. She was our first child, in a sense, making us into a little family of three, and she lived with us for five years before we had our children. Stormy lived to be 18 years of age. My girls, Mackenzie and Sianna, grew up with her and loved her as part of our family and were very attached to her as well.

Over time, the girls each adopted cats of their own that hung out with them most of the time, but I had a special bond with Stormy. She would sleep with us on our bed, snuggle, and give me lots of love. I always babied her, loved her, paid special attention to her and gave her treats. I was really connected to Stormy. She was a very vocal cat, very talkative and would talk to me a lot in her own way! She even seemed like a mother figure to my daughters' cats in some way. When they were kittens, both females from the same litter, Stormy seemed to take to them very well.

Stormy would even hang out with me when I was doing mediumship readings. When people would come over for a reading, I would have to ask them if they were allergic to cats. She would always hang out with me when I was meditating and praying in preparation for my sessions. She seemed to be drawn to that type of energy.

Eventually, when she was very old, she got really sick and lost a tremendous amount of weight. We realized that she was getting ready to make her journey home to the spirit world. I spoke to my children, telling them how much Stormy needed our prayers and our love, telling them that it was important to speak to her and support her by telling her it was okay to go.

After watching her struggle to breathe for about three hours, I wrapped her in a blanket to keep her warm. She could barely breathe, and she had a glazed look in her eyes, like she was between two worlds. I couldn't stand seeing her like that anymore, so I told the children that I had decided to compassionately help Stormy make her journey home. I didn't want her to continue to suffer anymore. I held her in my arms, bundled in a blanket, while my wife drove us all to the veterinary clinic nearby. Stormy hated going to the vet, so I didn't want her to feel stressed until it was absolutely necessary to go inside the clinic. I waited in the car with her and my girls while their mother went inside to make the arrangements.

As we were sitting in the car waiting, a bird came and landed on our windshield wiper and just stayed there, looking in at us. I understood that the little bird was acting as a messenger. My daughters asked, "Daddy, why is this little bird staring at us through the window?" I told them that the spirits were there with us to help guide Stormy home to the spirit world. The bird had no fear as it looked at us and our cat. Even though birds and cats don't normally get along, I told them, "It is here because it can see all the spirits in the spirit world and to let us know that Stormy will not be alone as she makes her journey home to the spirit world."

When my wife emerged from the clinic, I went in alone with Stormy in my arms, and I asked the vet what would be the most compassionate way to send her home to the spirit world. The vet explained the process to me: giving her gas to help her fall asleep before injecting the euthanasia medication. I said that I wanted to do it. I didn't want anyone else to send my cat to the spirit world. I wanted to be the one who would send her home. It happened quickly. I cried, my wife cried, my kids cried. It was a really, really difficult thing to do.

After we received her ashes, I placed them in a box and dug a spot for her in the place that she loved to spend time in all her life. Even though we don't live there anymore and I'm sure we don't hang around with our bodies once we have left them, I thought, *What better spot to place her remains than the place where she spent the majority of her life and where she was greatly loved?* The girls and I said a few words before we buried her ashes. We told her we loved her and that we couldn't think of a better place to lay her ashes than there. That is where she spent most of her life and we wanted her to know that whether we were still living there or not, we wanted to leave her in a space that was special for her. It was a very hard thing to do to let Stormy go, and just as we love our human family, it is also very true that we love our pets as family as well.

They teach us about love and compassion, friendship and companionship and protection. I'm so grateful for all the pets I've had in my life. In this journey of understanding the Animal Nation, I think they've all been teachers to me, whether it was the skunk, the rabbit, Charlie, Weasley, or Stormy. Stormy probably made the most impact because I don't think I've ever loved a cat before as much as I loved her. She lived a very long and full life. I wouldn't see Stormy again for many years after that day, until one of my spirit guides brought her through to visit me.

CHAPTER 5

♦ ♦ ♦ ♦

Wais+sk Jiksu'k, Jijaqmijk Saputita'jik

ANIMAL FAMILY, SPIRIT CONNECTIONS

Animals come to us in all forms. Whether they walk on all fours and have fur, crawl or slither along the ground, or fly around and have feathers, they all play a role in our life, providing us with companionship during times of great sorrow, through sickness, to help us get well, and just bringing us joy and happiness every day. They even cross over into the spirit world and continue their bond with us there. The Animal Nation is so linked to our family lives, and each of these animals is so important to us, that I have done readings for clients whose beloved pets in the spirit world have come through in the readings.

One of those clients was a man who had only one loved one in the spirit world, and it was his pet poodle. He didn't want to talk to anyone else. He brought pictures of his poodle for me to connect to his spirit. It is just amazing to see the incredible bond that people can and do have with their animal family.

While doing a different reading at a live session in Wolfville, Nova Scotia, a man came through. This man had apparently died in an accident while driving an all-terrain vehicle. While he was driving, his pet German shepherd was riding along with him on the back of it. When I connected to this man, who I'll call Andy, someone in the room stood up and said, "That's for me; it was my friend who died in a four-wheeler accident. He had his dog with him when he died." Shortly after the accident, Andy's German shepherd had also passed away.

While I was doing this session for the audience in Wolfville, everyone could hear a dog bark. It came through the actual PA system as I was making a connection to this man, Andy. I also connected to his dog and was validating that the dog was with him when a bark came through at the same time. Mind you, there was only a mixer and my mic hooked up with the guest mics, yet everybody in attendance had heard the dog bark. I reiterated to everybody that sometimes when I relay spirit messages, I can get audible validation from Spirit, sometimes people, about specific things, and in this case, the spirit of Andy's dog came through.

On another occasion, I was giving a private reading for a couple who came to me in hopes of making a connection to their son who had been murdered. The young man was talking to me in my mind about his two dogs named Yoshi and Yogi. There was also a voice in the background of that recording that said audibly, "tattoo." The spirit of the man wanted me to talk about a tattoo. The young man's mother hadn't gotten it yet but had been thinking about getting a tattoo! During the session, their son kept repeating these two names, "Yoshi and Yogi," which sounded kind of weird to me.

I asked the parents who they were, and they said those were the names of the two dogs that they used to have that had passed away. I did see two dogs with their son, but I couldn't put the reference together to Yoshi and Yogi right away. I told them that their son wanted them to know that they were with him and that he was able to spend time with them in the spirit world. Just as it is important for us to have a physical connection to our animals here on Earth, it is also as important for us to have a spiritual connection to our animals in the spirit world as well.

There was another reading that comes to mind, which was on my television show, *Spirit Talker*. I have done five seasons of *Spirit Talker*, and it happened during the filming of Season 3, Episode 3, while I was in Michipicoten First Nation, on the shores of Lake Superior. A man named David came to me with his wife and mother-in-law, hoping to connect to his wife's late father, but surprisingly, his dog came through first. I had sensed a father's energy near this man, the father of his father, who had died before David was even born. This man was watching over David and knew him. He brought along the spirit of a dog that had passed.

I felt this dog come through big time! There was such an incredible and profound bond between David and his dog that tears sprang to his eyes the minute I connected with her. She was a black Lab and Shar-Pei mix, around 60 pounds, and she was very intelligent. The man used to talk to his dog, and she would listen and would seem to understand, just like a human. Unfortunately she got very sick, and there was nothing that could be done to help her, so David had to make the decision to have her put down.

I could see into the dog's eyes for a second. I told David that pets are equally in the spirit world when they die as we humans are. The connection between pets and humans can be a strong one. They are our family, whether they are a dog, a cat, or any other pet that we love.

The dog showed me that the man had gotten a tattoo in memory of his beloved dog. It was a paw print on his leg, and

David rolled up his pant leg to show it to me. The dog wanted me to acknowledge that tattoo and let David know that she loved it! Then her energy went away, and I continued with the reading for the family.

Pets are connected to me and my people just as much as they are to my clients and their families. My cat Stormy, who would hang around me while I was giving readings at my home, would even pick up on the spirit energy of people's pets, because her ears would perk up whenever they would come through in a reading.

Many years after Stormy's passing, my spirit guide Eliza would come to me in a dream. Although I'd always thought of Stormy and remembered her, I never really experienced a profound spiritual connection to Stormy after her passing. I never had a visitation dream of her until much later in life when Eliza, a fairly new guide in spirit who I have come to know, came to me in a dream with Stormy so that I could have a moment with her. It was a completely unexpected visitation, a big surprise.

We were in a room that was all white, and in this room, Eliza appeared. She is an enormously smart, beautiful, vibrant, intelligent woman who I didn't even know was one of my guides until roughly around this time. She was wearing a long white robe, and she had on a necklace with a medallion and an amethyst set in the middle of it. Once I made the connection to her, she then brought my cat to visit me.

When I realized that Eliza had Stormy in her arms, I thought, *Oh my God, Stormy! I haven't seen you in so long!* I got to hold her and gave her the biggest hug that I could, but even in the spirit world, even though she loved me, she jumped right down after what seemed like five minutes and walked right through the wall into another dimension. I was only allowed to be with her for a short period of time in the spirit world, but I got the impression that there was another place for her to be. Then I looked at Eliza, I thanked her, and I woke up.

It was a short visit, but it was very profound, because I had never seen, held, or felt Stormy since the day that I unfortunately had to put her down. I had always wanted a visitation to take place, but I was never given the opportunity to have that moment with her until Eliza brought her through to me. I had the impression, though, that Stormy had a place to go in the spirit world. She had lived her life with me and now, wherever she was in the spirit world, it was the place she needed to be.

It reminded me of a teaching of Yeshua in the Bible, when he said, "There are many rooms in my Father's house; I would not tell you this if it were not true. I am going there to prepare a place for you." (John 14:1-3) The visitation took place in a room, one of those rooms Yeshua was referring to. Stormy was able to go through the wall to another dimension, but I couldn't follow her there. She moved back into the light, through the veil, and I was not able to see her anymore or sense her presence like I had just a moment before. If there is a room or a place to be for all spirits in the Creator's house, then there is also a place for animals.

When we go home to the spirit world, we will be reunited with all our pets and all our people, generations of people that we have known—family, friends, ancestors from previous lifetimes and also all of the pets that we have been connected to in this current lifetime and in previous lifetimes that will be there for that experience as well. It is so overwhelming to think of the big picture. In the meantime, before I make my journey home to the spirit world, I know that Stormy is not alone and that she is with her animal family in a place where animals are at peace, in a place where they need to be. Animals all have their own evolutionary process and personalities that they have to work through karmically that are formed and shaped through their many lifetimes too.

We just got a new puppy, a brown-and-black dachshund that I named Obi-Wan after the *Star Wars* character, and this puppy reminds me of another dog that we had when I was much younger. Maybe that puppy has come back in the form of Obi-Wan to work out the karma that he never got to work out last time, because the dog I used to have as a boy was a bit cross. He was not good with discipline and bit me once. He would attack us, and we couldn't trust him. But he died tragically—a car hit him.

When I met this new dog, Obi-Wan, the first time I held him, I had a feeling of having known him before. I was thinking of this other dog that had died. I have this sense of familiarity, that Obi-Wan has been in my life before and that maybe because he wasn't well in the past that perhaps he's been given another chance to be with me in my life, but he has come into this lifetime with a different temperament.

This new dog, Obi-Wan, seems stubborn and will likely be more difficult to raise than his brother, Scout, but he is loving and caring. He's insecure and can't stand to be alone. He will yelp and yelp for over an hour if he goes into his crate. He sleeps with us every night now because I can't sleep with him yelping so much. Perhaps we are working out karma together, and it is bringing us closer.

Animals have to evolve spiritually, just as humans do, and maybe there is unfinished karma that we have to work out together. Our pets, just like humans that are in our life, come to us with a soul contract, a purpose, to help us grow and learn about ourselves. It is not just us, as humans, taking care of our animals. They also come to us to teach us something.

Reincarnation is an Indigenous belief in our culture, and we believe that all things have a spirit; everything that we see all around us all has a spirit: the rivers, the rocks, the trees, plants, animals and humans. In my oracle card deck, *Wisdom of the Elders Oracle*, there is a card called Milky Way, Spirit Road. In Indigenous culture, when we point up to the stars in the Milky Way, we believe we are all connected to the stars. There is truth to that. We are all Star People. Our stars created life within our world, and we are actually made of stardust.

We all come from the dust of stars that have previously passed. That's why we call the sun Grandfather Sun, because it has existed before us. The Creator helped co-create the Earth, Mother Earth. They would not exist if it weren't for the remnants of other stars that have gone on before. Supernovas exploded and turned into atoms and became part of the universe themselves.

Quantum entanglement is when particles are connected. No matter how far apart they are, they are still connected. In Indigenous teaching, when we look out at the Milky Way, we see that those stars are all Grandfather Suns, they are all our grandfathers, because they've all come before us. They were created from the remnants of stars that have passed, and they even helped create the star that gives us life today, our sun.

As Indigenous people, when we look out to the Milky Way, when we leave this physical life, we have the potential to live another life, not only within this world but maybe in another world in one of those many stars in the Milky Way. In this way, we are all connected. Sometimes we reconnect with our ancestors within this lifetime, and I believe Obi-Wan, my little dachshund puppy, is my old dog coming back to me.

CHAPTER 6

♦ ♦ ♦ ♦

Lnu'k aq Tel Kikjolti'tij Wais+sk

INDIGENOUS PEOPLE AND THEIR CONNECTION TO THE ANIMAL NATION

Up until my late 30s, I wasn't yet deeply connected with my Indigenous heritage. It was only when I moved back to Nova Scotia in my 30s that I started to learn about and connect to my culture much more than I ever had before.

I had learned some things growing up by talking to my grandma in Newfoundland, in Conne River, where she was from, but I had grown up not knowing much about my connection to the Animal Nation, apart from loving animals as pets. I did grow up knowing that I was Mi'kmaq because she would take me aside and tell me, "You know, you're Mi'kmaq, eh?"

When I would go back to Newfoundland to visit her, I would meet an Indigenous Elder, the Chief and spiritual leader of the Conne River, Newfoundland Miawpukek First Nation. I learned that we had long ago lost the heritage of the clan system. He taught me that a clan was a family. A clan system, like last names, existed before contact with European culture. We didn't have last names. We were from different clans and would be known as John of the Bear clan, for example, or Tom of the Deer clan. The Chief taught me that there are many clans or families within a tribe. He believed that although we had lost that knowledge for the most part, our people were from the Bear clan.

The Chief also told me that people from, for instance, the Bear clan could not marry and have children with someone else in the Bear clan, in order to keep the family lineage genetically healthy and strong. Beth of the Eagle clan, for example, once she came of age to begin courting, could not court or marry someone else from the Eagle clan. This was to avoid someone marrying a close relative like a first cousin, for instance.

I also learned that typically, Indigenous people from a clan do not eat the animal that is their clan animal. For example, Joe of the Deer clan would abstain from eating deer meat. It is a sign of respect to one's Animal Nation. Some people will still do it, but as a general rule, we do not eat a member of our clan. If people are not deeply connected to their culture, they don't really care. If they are more deeply connected to their culture, though, they may respect it more. They would not want to disrespect their clan totem.

I at least grew up knowing that we all belonged to a clan system, and that was all I knew at that point in my life about my culture. I knew I was Mi'kmaq; I identified as being of the Bear clan (and it was confirmed to me by some members of the Bear clan in Conne River) but that was about as great an understanding that I had in relation to my culture and connections to the Animal Nation. I was still trying to understand who I was as an Indigenous person. I had yet to meet several Indigenous Elders much later on in my life who would teach me so much more about the Animal Nation and about who I was.

I thought I had some special connection to the bear, and as it turns out, I really do, greater than I thought. It just so happened that the Bear clan wasn't just my clan name, but I also had a deep connection to the Bear Nation itself, specifically the Polar Bear Nation. I have since discovered that the Polar Bear is one of my Spirit Animals.

I didn't really know I had a Spirit Animal when I was young, but I had maybe gotten a hint that I had a special connection to the Bear Nation when my dog Weasley saved me from a young bear so many years ago. It went deeper than just having a Bear clan name, though. The possibility of a connection to the Bear Nation as my Spirit Animal as well became a little clearer to me after an experience in British Columbia that I will never forget.

Every year on June 21, the Full Moon in June adventure race takes place across British Columbia and Alberta, Canada. It is run in teams of four, with at least one person of the opposite sex on each team. We had to race 150 to 300 kilometers through the Rocky Mountains. I've done that race five times. These races take place in the mountains, rivers, lakes, and trails in various locations, and this one time it was near Kimberly, British Columbia.

When I was younger, I could run like the wind. I could do mountain climbing, mountain biking, canoeing, and hiking. Orienteering through the wilderness was not a problem for me. I was the fastest one on my team, and I was also the one who was responsible for orienteering through these races. The first part of this race was 50 kilometers. We had to orienteer by map and by compass, not by GPS, to get to certain coordinates or points on the map. This was to figure out where we had to be for our next transition in the race.

This race had around 40 teams, and our team was pretty much in the lead. There were many teams that were not that far behind us, because I could see the lights of the other runners' headlights bouncing along the trails and through the trees way off in the distance. I ran a few hundred yards ahead to keep the members of my team motivated to follow me and keep up. Of course, I wanted us to win the race.

I reached a clearing about 100 meters ahead of my team. As I was jogging through the area that had been burned by a forest fire a few years prior, I led my team through the clearing so we could get back onto the trail and continue our journey. My light was on my head so I could see more clearly. In spite of the light of the full moon, there was some cloud cover that night. It was very early in the race, probably around 3:30 in the morning.

I had slowed to a jog as I reached the clearing. I was suddenly aware of a red light shining back at me only about 20 feet away. I continued jogging, all the while staring at that red light, wondering what it might be from. My first thought was that it couldn't be eyes, because there was only one and it was much too high up to be anything alive. I thought it might be a bit of reflective tape on a tree. I thought there must have been at least one tree still standing in the burned-out clearing, because for anything to be that high up, it had to be a tree, and someone must have put something reflective on it so we wouldn't run into it.

As I got closer, I realized there were two lights, not just one. I still thought that they couldn't be eyes because they were spaced around a foot apart. So I unsuspectingly got closer and closer until I was only a few feet away when it finally dawned on me that this was not reflective tape at all but actually eyes reflecting the light from my headlamp. This was a bear!

Suddenly, he stood up on his hind legs; he was the biggest grizzly bear that I had ever seen in my entire life! However big a grizzly can get, that was as big as he was. Despite thinking that I was Indigenous and that the bear was part of my clan, I was absolutely terrified. I thought, *I am bear meat. There's nowhere to go, there are no trees to get behind or climb, I don't have anything to defend myself with.* I had seen other grizzlies before at different times, in valleys and on mountains, but this one was the biggest I had ever seen. I had never seen one this close up either. I could smell him. I could smell his breath, and I could feel his breath as he moved a little bit closer to me, sniffing the air to smell me. I was terrified for my life. I thought, *Okay. This is it.* I was having a near-death experience, because I really thought, *I'm going to die here. I am not going to survive this.*

My knowledge of what to do when confronted by bears was not to startle them, and since it was dark, I knew he couldn't see me very well. He could obviously see my headlamp as it shone right at him. The only thing I could think of doing was to wave my arms in front of me and talk to the bear while I walked backward and he moved slowly toward me. I said, "Hey, bear, I don't mean you any harm. I'm not here to harm you in any way. I'm just walking." I even told him, "I'm part of the Bear clan, and I'm not going to taste very good. We're from the same clan, so I wouldn't eat you. Don't eat me."

I also knew from my bear safety training course that if I was in a group of four and met a bear, the chances of dying in a bear attack were slim. That many people in a group are much less likely to get attacked and killed by a bear than a lone hiker. I called out to the rest of my team, "Hey, guys, can you come here?" "Why?" they called back. "Just come now, please."

When my team caught up to me, they all shone their headlights in front of them, and then they saw what was directly in front of me, the biggest bear that had ever lived! They said, "Why would you call us to come near you?" Everyone was afraid. "If we are all together, we are less likely to be attacked," I replied. One of the members of our group was supposed to have been carrying the can of bear spray because it was a required item to do the race, but when I asked her for it, she said, "I did not bring the bear spray." I said, "What do you mean, you didn't bring the bear spray?" She told me that she had removed it earlier in order to lighten her backpack, not thinking that we would ever need it. I said, "Why would you not bring it? It's supposed to be with us on every leg of the race." We all waved our arms in the air and backed away slowly from the giant bear.

She and her husband, who were both French, suggested we should sing to the bear to keep him calm, so we all started singing the song, "Frere Jacques, Frere Jacques, dormez-vous, dormez-vous . . ." while we were waving our arms in front of us. The grizzly just kept standing there, sniffing the air to get a good whiff of us, then dropped down on all fours and got within 10 feet of us as he walked past us and up the hill behind us!

I knew that I had a connection to the bear, and even though it was the scariest encounter with a bear that I had ever had in my life, I also felt oddly safe. When he walked by us, I realized he was not interested in eating us. If he had wanted to eat me, he would have eaten me before my team arrived. I had probably disturbed him in his sleep, and he had one eye open, wondering what the heck was coming down the hill. As I got closer to him, he had to open both his eyes to get a better look at me. He got up on his hind legs because he probably thought I was the one who was there to hurt him! He sniffed and got a good whiff of all of us as he stood up on his hind legs. He didn't want any trouble.

He kept on walking up the hill as the other teams in the race, about 30 of them, ran down the hill behind us, and he parted the runners like Moses parting the Red Sea. He just kept right on walking, not interested in any of them. Not one person was injured that night by that grizzly bear. Afterward, the other runners would exclaim, "Did you see that bear?" I think I was the first person to see him.

I know that the bear had a special connection to me, in a way, even then, but I wasn't yet convinced that the bear was my Power Totem Animal at that stage in my life. I felt that it was very significant; I was meant to meet this bear and have this bear encounter, and I was meant to have it alone, for a few moments at least. I wouldn't run out and try to do it again, but I knew that this was meant to happen. I didn't realize how significant my connection to the bear was until much later in life. I wasn't yet very knowledgeable about the totems at that point, but I would find out soon enough.

CHAPTER 7

♦ ♦ ♦ ♦

We'jitasik Mpisun Wejiaq Wape'k Mestapekiejit

DISCOVERING THE MEDICINE OF THE WHITE BUFFALO

There might have been Animal Medicine that had been with me throughout my life, but I couldn't yet fully identify it. There were hints of it, though, like the bear incidents. It wasn't until I started to recognize these medicines within my life that I started to see that there was a purpose in having them. I would still need to learn about the four directions of my Indigenous culture and all of the teachings that went along with that knowledge. There were also deep connections between the Medicine Wheel and the different stages of life, and corresponding Animal Medicines that would come to me in these various stages.

After moving back east to Nova Scotia, I met an Algonquin gentleman named Andre, a native French speaker who spoke heavily accented English. He was a medicine carrier and a psychic medium and minister for the Spiritualist Church, and he was offering a course. Andre was the first person who introduced me to Animal Medicine when he gifted me my first medicine to carry with me through life.

I was interested in learning more about my gifts and how I could use them. I wanted to move away from just doing private readings and felt compelled to be in front of people in some way. I had been doing one-on-one readings for a very long time in Calgary. I did once teach a course there, and people were very receptive to that. When I moved back East, the predominant work that I did was as a psychic medium who just happened to be Indigenous, but I felt a calling to step into doing that work more fully.

I felt nudged by Spirit to attend a Spiritualist Church. There were people there who were doing readings, so I went down there and introduced myself. I asked if it would be all right if I volunteered to give a talk and also do some readings. I knew that they allowed people to do this, because whenever I was there, I saw that they would bring in guests.

One of the guests was Andre. He was a spiritualist minister who was giving readings there. He was offering a workshop on the weekend. I went to see Andre do sessions in front of people, and I was inspired by him because he seemed to be more connected to his culture than I was. He resonated with me because here was a fellow Indigenous man, not Mi'kmaq but Algonquin, and the Mi'kmaq people speak a dialect of the Algonquin language. We are all connected as Indigenous people. He was also a psychic medium, and I thought, *Maybe I can learn something from him.*

I ended up attending one of his workshops, which was inspired by Indigenous principles. People were seated in a circle, and there were what he called different doors in the circle, representing East, South, West, and North. He invited me to sit in the Eastern door because the Mi'kmaq people are known as the people of the land of the dawn. We are from the easternmost point of Turtle Island.

This ceremony was held indoors in a hall, and he began by smudging us all, using the smoke of the smudge to cleanse our spirits and auras. I had smudged in my lifetime, but I wasn't very knowledgeable about it. I didn't even know yet how to do it properly according to Indigenous tradition. Even so, he allowed me to smudge myself.

Andre lit sacred candles and placed them around a clear quartz crystal cluster that rested on a tripod that looked like a real fire (I would later learn that traditional ceremonies would have a real fire). He explained to me that the crystal would amplify the intentions of everyone who was there, seated around this representation of a traditional sacred fire.

We did the ceremony, and there were four rounds, which was very true to Indigenous tradition. We would talk to Spirit in different ways, and we would all channel Spirit. We would all give messages that we were receiving from Spirit. Every person in the whole circle had a turn, about 25 to 30 people in all. Andre would choose different people to stand in the different Cardinal Directions.

There were four energy holders for each of the four directions of the wheel, and he had chosen me to stand up and represent the Eastern door of the wheel because he had heard about me from the others and about my work doing readings as a psychic medium. Andre was standing in the Southern door, and two other people were standing in the Western and the Northern doors.

After the service, Andre approached me and said, "I have a gift for you. I feel I have to give you this, and I think it's medicine that you're meant to carry." He gave me a little glass bead, and inside the glass were the ashes of a white buffalo. He gifted it to me. He had been given a few of these, and he carried some of that medicine for himself. He felt that I also needed to carry that medicine—that Animal Medicine—in life.

I thanked him for it, and after the ceremony, I told him how much I liked the sacred fire with the crystals and the candles in the middle of the circle. To my great pleasure and surprise, he said, "You know what, Shawn, I think you should carry that too." He gave me the crystal fire, which I still have to this day in my office in Nova Scotia. The clear quartz crystal cluster rests on the tripod in my workspace and is part of the medicine that I carry. I had never been gifted quartz by anybody before then. The fact that I had been so drawn to the clear quartz, and that Andre told me it would amplify my work in life, meant that it was very special, so I've kept that sacred fire.

I knew I had a connection to the buffalo at that point, but it was still very much like the Bear Medicine that I had encountered in the woods. It wasn't clear to me as a totem of mine until much later in life. Andre told me about a prophecy and how the medicine of the white buffalo would change and shift the world, but I had never heard about these things before. I promised him that I would carry that medicine, but I hadn't yet identified that the buffalo was a totem of mine.

Back then, I didn't know who I was, just like many people who don't yet know who they are either, but there are hints of who our Animal Totems that are walking with us through life might be. Some of these medicines might be coming to us in weird and unexpected ways, such as my two chance encounters of bears in the woods and someone gifting me the ashes of a white buffalo. I have also been gifted a buffalo rattle made of buffalo hide by a woman named Linda in British Columbia, who made it and sent it to me. More of these would make themselves known to me as I learned more about my Indigenous culture. These Totem Animals were always with me throughout my life, but I hadn't yet discovered that they were walking with me.

Very soon after this workshop, the Spiritualist Church asked me to come back and do my own talks and give readings for people in the audience, which I did. They embraced me and this is what catapulted me locally. When I started attending the Spiritualist Church, there was hardly anyone there, but once I started doing readings there, the attendance doubled. Whenever I would give readings, the hall would be full. People were interested in coming to hear me speak and do sessions. Some of the ministers there were even coming to me for guidance about mediumship. It was very apparent to everyone there that I had a clear grasp on the universal language of spirit and communication that would come through to people like mediums.

Eventually, though, I felt that it was not the space that I was meant to progress in. Sadly, some egos were involved, and because of some of that within the Spiritualist Church, I decided to step away and walk on my own journey. I needed to be who I was and not what others were. I had not been looking for a church. I was just looking for a place to express myself and learn about myself, stepping more into the light as a psychic medium. I was a bit scared to do that, because I hadn't done anything publicly before, and the Spiritualist Church allowed me to feel like I could start to move out more into the public eye rather than just giving private readings for people as I had been doing up until then.

I set up my first show and sold about 100 tickets. It was the first time people actually came and paid to see me. It was an amazing feeling. I felt that because I was part of the ceremony with Andre the Algonquin, and the things I had learned about myself as an Indigenous person, I was inspired by him to get out there and learn more and reveal more of who I was to the public.

The medicine of the White Buffalo is about showing respect and being shown respect within the community. I teach about this in my oracle card deck, *Wisdom of the Elders Oracle*, as one of the Seven Grandfather Teachings. The medicine of the Bison and Buffalo relates to the concept of Respect. In the deck, I described that "Indigenous people built a sustainable relationship with Buffalo upon a foundation of mutual respect . . . [I was] being shown a deeper level of respect within [my] own community." I was also entering a new and healthier phase of my life, learning about and respecting more and more of my own Indigenous culture.

I feel like the medicine of the White Buffalo coming to me at that time, even though I didn't identify it as being a Totem Animal for me just yet, helped me through that period of my life as I became a more public figure and was being shown respect for what I did. When I researched the medicine of the White Buffalo, I became aware that carrying it was helping me to gain more respect within the Spiritualist Church. Then eventually it helped me when stepping out on my own to become my own person. Even though I was not fully aware of the Bison as my totem, the medicine of the Bison was definitely working with me as I carried it in life.

Eventually, I became aware that carrying Animal Medicine would help me as an Indigenous person through the different phases in my life. I didn't relate the carrying of medicine to having those animals as my totems, though, which is a deeper connection than just having the medicines come to me. The White Buffalo Medicine that I received from Andre inspired me to learn more about my Indigenous culture, and I prayed for Spirit to send me someone, an Elder, who could teach me more about who I was as an Indigenous person, and this would come to me in a most unexpected way.

CHAPTER 8

♦ ♦ ♦ ♦

We'ju't Kisiku

FINDING AN ELDER

Since receiving the White Buffalo Medicine, I have been working more in the public eye. My first experience with Andre was pretty energizing for me. It was a breath of fresh air in a sense because nobody had ever gifted me anything before in regard to Animal Medicine. It inspired me to reach out to learn more.

I had always sensed that I had a connection to the Eagle Nation, but I didn't know yet if it was one of my totems or not. I thought that maybe I had a connection to the eagle just because I was an Indigenous person, and eagles are very important to our culture.

One day, as I was canoeing down the Shubenacadie River in Nova Scotia, just enjoying the day, this one eagle was flying continuously overhead. This wasn't unusual—I would often see eagles while canoeing. I felt that it was a female eagle. As it continued to fly overhead, I spoke to her. I said, "Well, if you're going to keep flying over my head, I would really appreciate a feather."

As she flew overhead many times, coming so close to me that I could feel the wind from her wings rushing through my hair, I thought she might use her talons to take the hair off my head! That's how close she came to me. Maybe she never got that close, but it felt like it, because they are such large birds with such a large wingspan.

After flying over my head, she would perch herself in a tree and watch me go by, doing this again and again. I would canoe farther down the river as she watched me, then she would fly over my head and perch on a branch in the next tree. I thought, *What is this eagle trying to do? Is she trying to protect a nest, or is she protecting an area and trying to scare me off?*

I continually spoke to the eagle, saying, "Hey, if you're going to keep on doing this, I would love to have a feather, because I am Indigenous and eagles are very important to my people, and if you want me to carry your medicine as well as the Buffalo Medicine, then I'd appreciate a feather."

As Indigenous people, the eagle is very special. It is important to us because it is used in the celebration of Indigenous culture. At any powwow, or Mawio'mi, as it's called in Mi'kmaq, everybody is wearing eagle feathers. *Mawio'mi* is a Mi'kmaq word, which translates to "gathering." Many First Nations communities all across Canada celebrate their culture this way. During a Mawio'mi, people sing, dance, and drum. Their headdresses, their sacred items, things that they carry, have eagle feathers all over them, and here I was, an Indigenous person, and I didn't even have an eagle feather! I almost felt like I was not Indigenous. I had nothing. I didn't want to go out and ask an Elder if I could have an eagle feather, because it has to be gifted to you or come to you in some way. I thought, *What better person to ask for this medicine than the eagle itself?*

After the twelfth time that she flew over my head, sure enough, I saw a feather fall from her and float down the river. I paddled over as quickly as I could and picked up the feather. It was my very first eagle feather! She was a young eagle, not yet mature, so there was some brown in the coloring and she still had some spots and different colors. There was also a big piece missing out of the feather that looked like it was cut out. One side of the feather looked good, but the other

Finding an Elder

side didn't. As I picked it up out of the water, she watched me from the tree. I called up to her and said, "Listen, I appreciate the feather, but can you give me a better one?"

Then she looked at me and just flew off, as if to say, "How dare you? I dropped this feather for you, and you don't appreciate it! You didn't ask me for the *best* feather I own, you just said you wanted *a* feather! I gave you one of the feathers that I could afford to lose, so here's some medicine, take it, and stop being so disrespectful!" That's what I felt she was saying to me. Nevertheless, I carried that Eagle Medicine with me from then on.

Sometime after that, I did an event at the Veith House in Halifax. It is a place in town for parents who are disconnected from their children, to give them visitation rights if they've been taken away. I was asked by the Veith House to do a charity event to raise funds for the children it served. Since it is a nonprofit organization that is providing a service to the community, I was happy to do it. Although it was government funded, they still needed money for many things that they did not have a budget for. They sold tickets to the event and also had a 50-50 draw and other things going on in the hall to raise money.

As I was doing the event, I noticed a lady in the front row. I looked at her, and I unexpectedly connected to four people who were murdered, but who were not directly related to her. I said, "I have four missing and murdered Indigenous people that are coming through to me." I could see that it was somewhere in Cape Breton and somewhere on the side of a hill near the Bras d'Or Lake. I asked her, "Do you know anything about these people?"

She said that she had just learned of them the week before, because somebody had told her the story about those people. I said, "They're connected to somebody named Joe. If you tell Joe, I might be able to give him some guidance in regard to finding his family. I can tell him what happened to them and where they are." It so happened that it was a cold case that Joe, a retired Royal Canadian Mounted Police officer, had been working on for years. It was his missing grandparents and great-aunt and great-uncle who came through to me during the show.

The woman looked like she was Mi'kmaq to me, but I wasn't 100 percent sure. After the event was over, she came up to me, and I learned that her name was Cathy. I connected to her, and she asked me a question about her son who was lost. I talked to her about her son for a brief time, and then she asked me, "Shawn, are you Mi'kmaq? You definitely look Mi'kmaq; you must have some ancestry there." I told her that my grandmother was Mi'kmaq. She replied, "I knew it! I knew you were Mi'kmaq. I could tell you were."

I wasn't publicly celebrating who I was just then as a Mi'kmaq person while doing events or during my readings, but I carried the medicine of the Eagle and the White Buffalo when I was doing sessions. It made a difference to me personally—I felt more connected to my heritage with the Medicine close to me. Being Indigenous was just part of who I was as a person as opposed to my being connected to the culture publicly. I told her about my grandmother in Newfoundland and about being disconnected from my culture and my language. Cathy told me that she also knew the Chief from Newfoundland, where my grandmother was from, and that she had done some photography and some filming with him. I told her that I had actually prayed, after meeting Andre, that I would meet someone that I could learn from. She took down my contact information and very shortly afterward, within a week or two, as I was staying in Nova Scotia, someone came knocking at my door.

It was an Elder by the name of Joe. He was very well respected in the community and very connected to his culture. He said, "I heard that you want to learn about culture." I didn't make the connection right away that this was the Joe I had gotten a message for during the show, because I forget things that I say in the moment. He was intrigued about what I had said to Cathy about his missing family members, but he also was very sincere in his willingness to teach me about my culture.

I sat with Joe, and he spoke to me for a long time. He taught me how to smudge properly and so many other things. He brought out his eagle wing, which he kept wrapped in red cloth, and taught me what a bundle was and the importance of wrapping my sacred objects in one. He talked to me about Eagle Medicine, and I showed him my eagle feather that I had just gotten. I told him how I had received it, and he said that it was very special and that even the missing piece in it meant something. It was missing a piece just as a piece of my culture was still missing and wasn't yet filled in. I was very intrigued by what he was telling me about culture, and he eventually took me to different sweat ceremonies and talking circles.

He even brought me to New Brunswick once, to help with an event, a talking circle, for three Royal Canadian Mounted Police officers who were killed in Moncton, New Brunswick. He brought me there to do the talking ceremony for him and the families of the officers who were lost. One of the wives was Indigenous, and Joe had been working on her healing process. I learned a lot about culture through Joe and his teachings.

Once we had gotten to know each other well, Joe asked me if I had my Indigenous name, and I said, "No. I know that there are a lot of people who have Indigenous names, but I was never gifted one." My grandmother didn't have one, but she knew about being from the Bear clan. Other than that, there was no knowledge about any other names that had been given. Joe paused, and then expressed that he intended to give me a name. He said, "We're going to do a little ceremony."

During the ceremony he seemed to go into a bit of a trance. When he came out of the trance, he said, "From now on, you're going to be called White Eagle Spirit Talker." That's when I was given my Indigenous name: Wape'k Kitpu Aknutmajik Jijaqmij. He told me that it was not just my name but also reflected the deep connection I had to the Eagle itself and that I was meant to carry the Eagle Medicine.

It clicked for me: I had been given signs that my future name might include Eagle, because that summer in Newfoundland, I had found three other eagle feathers. They were all white tail feathers. I never told Joe about the white feathers that I found until after the naming ceremony. Joe confirmed that it was no accident that I was named White Eagle. After meeting Cathy, Joe, and all of the synchronicities with the eagle feathers, I knew that White Eagle Spirit Talker was meant to be my Indigenous name. These are the types of synchronicities that we should pay special attention to. If an animal or its energy appears in our lives, we know that the medicine is coming to us.

Joe then brought the eagle wing that he had shown me on his first visit to my house and gifted it to me after giving me my Indigenous name. He told me that I was to use it in my life, to use that medicine of the Eagle to help and serve others. I said, "But this is yours, Joe. I can't take this from you." He said, "I'll get another one. I have carried the medicine of your wing for a long time, and it was gifted to me by another Elder. You are meant to carry this from now on." It was a great honor to receive that eagle wing, and it is still part of my sacred bundle and an important part of the Eagle Medicine that I carry with me through life.

CHAPTER 9

♦ ♦ ♦ ♦

To'tmk Pana'lsultijik

TOTEMS REVEAL THEMSELVES

Even though I was gifted the Eagle Medicine, I was given my Indigenous name, I knew I was part of the Bear clan, and bears had shown up in my life, it wasn't until I had a very profound dream that everything changed for me. That dream not only shifted my whole awareness around Animal Medicines and how they'd been with me in the past, but also, it made me aware that they were totems that had always been a part of my life. My epiphany came with the dream of the white polar bear, or Wapek Muin.

In the dream, I was in the middle of a field, and for some reason there were seven shadows chasing me and trying to do me harm. I believe now that it was a prophetic dream, because there would be seven members of a family causing me a lot of trouble legally in the near future. Looking back on it now, I see things more clearly.

I was running down the field away from these seven shadowy figures, and I didn't know why I was running from them, only that they were going to do me harm in some way. Then when I looked across the field, there was a forest on the other side of the clearing. Out of the forest came seven polar bears. All I could think was that I was trying to outrun these seven shadowy people who were trying to do me harm, and suddenly I was faced with these seven polar bears that were probably just going to eat me!

I thought I had a better chance of outrunning the people, so I started running toward them, and suddenly they also turned and were all running away from the polar bears that were coming toward all of us. I was running for my life. At some point, I realized that I couldn't outrun them all, and I surrendered to the polar bears. I believed they were going to hurt me and potentially eat me. I surrendered to the thought that this was going to happen.

What happened instead was that the seven polar bears ran past me and pounced on each of the shadowy figures. The shadows just disintegrated. They were not real people; they were just energy. As each polar bear hopped onto the shadows, they would just vanish into the light of the polar bears themselves. They didn't devour them, didn't do them harm, but it was their energy and their light that protected me and overcame the darkness that the shadowy figures were carrying. All seven of the bears then turned around and they melded into one great polar bear.

They were from the Polar Bear Nation, and I already knew from my grandmother and from talking to the Chief of Conne River that I was connected to the Bear Nation. I knew that the Bear was part of my clan, but it wasn't just my clan name, it was actually a protection and medicine that had been part of my life all along. It wasn't apparent until that moment, when the polar bears merged into one great bear that looked at me with great compassion and wisdom in its eyes, that I realized the bears were there to protect me.

I knew, in the dream, in a kind of epiphany, that the bears weren't there to hurt me. They were there to keep me safe. I realized then that this was a totem and that there had been hints of this totem showing up throughout my life. The Bear Nation was my medicine, but the Polar Bear Nation in particular, or Wapek Muin, was my Power Totem Animal.

This realization brought me to the knowledge that not only do I carry Eagle Medicine, but also that the Eagle is one of my totems. I psychically knew that each of the medicines was uniquely different. The Eagle Medicine was more of a Spirit Totem Animal that guided me in a good way in how I approached people in life as a heart-centered spirit talker and psychic medium.

In my life journey, I have faced many people, and sometimes not so good ones. I've been through a few difficult situations with people in the past, and I feel like the Polar Bear was like a Power Totem Animal that was protecting me. The medicine of the Great White Polar Bear was one of my totems in regard to protection. As far as I was aware at that point in my life, there was a Power Totem Animal and a Spirit Totem Animal. I was aware that I had two distinct ones. I wasn't yet 100 percent sure of my other totems, though, until I started filming my television show, *Spirit Talker.*

Just as I had received gifts from the Eagle Nation, like the wing feather, the tail feathers, and the eagle wing from my friend and mentor Elder Joe, I came into possession of gifts from the Polar Bear Nation, too. Shortly after my dream, I prayed to the Creator for something from the polar bear to carry with me through life. My prayer was answered when a friend and Spirit Talker Tribe student named Barbara presented me with a bear claw that was made into a necklace. It had been gifted to her by an Inuit Elder who said it was to be given to someone else. That someone was me. I wear that bear claw every day, close to my heart, and when I am not wearing it, I wrap it in a piece of polar bear fur that was gifted to me by a woman named Lori to keep it safe. I also came into possession of a polar bear fur rug, another gift from a woman named Jennifer. Then, quite unexpectedly, I recently came into possession of yet another polar bear rug.

Just near the end of writing this book, something amazing happened. It was on the eve of the winter solstice, 2024. I got a call from a woman named Kelly. The father of her husband, Steve, had unfortunately passed away some years ago, but while he was alive he had lived in the Northwest Territories. He had been looking for a polar bear rug at that time but there were not many around. Several Inuit people had them, so he managed to meet up with one Inuk fellow who had one that was in pristine condition, with the full back of the polar bear, its magnificent head still intact and the claws on its paws as well. It was a massive bear, over 10 feet long and just as wide. The Inuk Elder had hunted it and cured its hide himself, so it was ethically sourced. This fellow really needed a new sled for his dogs, so he sold the rug to Steve's father. He kept the polar bear rug for many years, until his passing.

When Steve and Kelly were sorting through his father's personal items, they discovered the polar bear rug. Not knowing exactly what to do with it, they kept it in a closet for many years. When Kelly joined my Spirit Talker Tribe course, she heard about my polar bear story. She looked at her husband and they both decided where it was meant to go. They set up a meeting so they could gift me the polar bear rug.

After learning about the history of the rug, I promised them that I would honor and respect it as the fourth part of the seven polar bears that I have received in my life as my Power Totem Animal. I promised that I would keep it for the rest of my life and honor it, and now it lies on top of my pool table in my home. I look into his eyes, I touch his claws, I pet his fur, and I speak to him every day. That medicine is in my home, and it will remain in my home until the day I die. I just absolutely love it, and not because it's a trophy but because of the medicine that this great animal has brought into my life.

Strangely, when I look into the eyes of the bear, they look familiar to me. I have such a strong feeling that this is the same bear from my dream. It is like he knew me before I knew him, and I feel like this is the great polar bear that stood there when all the bears walked into one. This is the bear that looked me in the eye that day. His spirit has already been with me, but it just took time for the Great Spirit, the Creator, and some really nice people, Kelly and her husband, Steve, and also his sister, to decide to give that bear to me to hold, to honor, and to respect and work with his sacred medicine for the rest of my life.

Ever since that bear has come into my home, other magical, synchronistic things have been happening under my roof. In the same room as the bear, I have a clear quartz crystal ball sitting on a stand with a light underneath it. One day something hit the window, and I saw that the crystal ball was knocked off its stand. I was walking toward the window when I felt an energy move toward me, and I felt it just as the crystal ball fell into the wall. I feel it was the spirit of the bear.

Another thing that has happened is that my moose hide drum, which is up on a shelf in my office, wedged in there, made a sound. I was upstairs when I heard something that sounded like my drum. It's very hard to move and has to be pulled on to get it to move. When I came down to see what happened, it was tipped over. I have a clear quartz pillar just beside it, and the drum fell over and hit it and was leaning on it. So that makes two things connected to quartz that have happened since I got the polar bear rug. I find it unusual, and I'm sure it has to do with the spirit of the Great White Polar Bear, Wapek Muin.

Spirit never ceases to amaze me, because shortly after receiving that polar bear rug, a Spirit Talker Tribe member named John was in a shop with his wife and they came across a polar bear claw there. They thought it deserved to be brought home and turned into a necklace with some old beads that he had at home, which came from some Indigenous people who had given him a necklace at one time. That necklace broke, and John thought that if things break, they might not be meant to come back to him; they are meant to go to someone else. He put the polar bear claw and the beads together on a necklace and decided to gift it to me. It came to me in a little red pouch, with some sage medicine inside it as well. I received it while writing the last chapter of this book, just as I had received the giant white polar bear rug a few weeks before. Now, because of the alignment of all things, I have five of the seven Great White Polar Bear Medicines that I always knew would come into my life at the right moment. I appreciate this gift of a polar bear claw necklace, and I will treasure it, along with the four other polar bear gifts I have received in my lifetime, for the rest of my life, and I will use it in a good way.

I feel that in the future, I will come into possession of two more polar bear gifts, to represent all seven of the polar bears from my dream, but these will come to me all in good time. In the meantime, to honor the medicine of the Eagle and the Polar Bear, I have gotten a tattoo of each on my chest. On my right side, I have a polar bear claw, and on my left, an eagle. When I do live shows, I wear a white ceremonial ribbon shirt with beading of a bear claw and an eagle on the front over each of my tattoos. In this way, the Eagle Medicine and the Polar Bear Medicine always walk with me no matter where I go and also while I am in service to Spirit.

Animal Medicine follows everyone in life, whether they are Indigenous or non-Indigenous people, because we are all Indigenous to somewhere in the world and every nation carries its own sacred Animal Medicine. The Animal Nation walks with all of us, whether we are aware of it yet or not.

CHAPTER 10

◆ ◆ ◆ ◆

Jijaqmijk Kelulaji aq Wape'k Mestapekiejit

SPIRIT TALKER AND THE WHITE BUFFALO

Once it was apparent to me that I had at least two Totem Animals, and two different Animal Medicines that I was working with in very uniquely different ways, I realized that I was still on a journey of discovering who I really was. I wanted to learn more about which other totems might also be walking with me. Through that journey of discovery, I started to film a Canadian television program called *Spirit Talker* for APTN, Aboriginal Peoples Television Network.

Throughout my five seasons filming the show, I got to travel all across Canada to many Indigenous communities, and I learned so much about Indigenous culture, met many Elders, and incorporated many teachings from different Nations, not just Mi'kmaq teachings, into my cultural understanding. I felt that I had a prayer answered in relation to understanding who I was as an Indigenous person. When we pray, we should be careful what we ask for, because it might come through in a big way! My answer to prayer came through in the grandest way for me.

The show *Spirit Talker* is about me going to different communities and learning about culture for part of each episode, and the other part of each episode is about me doing sessions for people to help them receive messages from their loved ones in spirit. I helped different communities reconnect to their ancestors to overcome grief and loss, helping them move through life in a better way while they helped me reconnect to my Indigenous culture and teachings from the Elders.

During the filming of Season 4, Episode 2, I got to travel to a community in Sioux Valley Dakota First Nation, just outside of Brandon in Manitoba, Canada. It is part of a big Nation that extends to the United States. I got to meet Tony Tacan, an Elder in the community, who looks after a large buffalo herd next to his family ranch, along with his son. Buffalo is how Indigenous people refer to the Tatanka Nation, or as they are commonly known, the bison, a woodland or mountain buffalo. They are the caretakers and stewards of the buffalo in an effort to bring them back from near extinction. They keep over one hundred head of buffalo on the ranch. The Sioux Valley Dakota Nation owns the ranch on which the buffalo are kept, and Tony runs it in an effort to bring the buffalo back. Tony's father taught him that "if you take care of the animals, they're going to take care of you."

Tony shared with me how, in Indigenous culture, the buffalo has given so much to us in the past. The buffalo have taken care of their people for centuries, supplying them with hides for their teepees, bones for their tools and weapons, and also food for their sustenance. Buffalo provided them with that way of life, and now the community has a responsibility to take care of them in return.

Over a century ago, the buffalo were hunted nearly to extinction, being killed for their skins and then left to waste for no apparent reason. Indigenous people, however, would only hunt what they needed for their survival and would use every part of the buffalo without wasting anything that the animals had given in sacrificing their life for the community. Indigenous people respect the buffalo, and the buffalo teaches us respect, as I've mentioned in a previous chapter and also in my *Wisdom of the Elders Oracle* card deck. The buffalo have given us their life, their resources for our life, from their hides to their bones, and every part of the buffalo itself for our survival and well-being. Now we have an obligation, as the Sioux Valley peoples' Elder told me, to give life back to the buffalo just as they have given us life. We must now care for them in return.

Tony's son told me that a white buffalo was so rare, it was one in 10 million. The Winnipeg Zoo gifted them a white buffalo, along with her twin brother. Over the years, the number of white buffalo in their herd has grown to 11. The odds of a white buffalo coming into life are very small, and there is a prophecy about the white buffalo as well. It is significant that so many white buffalo are being born to that herd that is being taken care of, to share the message of the White Buffalo Calf Woman prophecy. It has to do with us taking care of the Animal Nation, the ecosystem, and the environment.

To the Dakota people, the white buffalo are sacred, held in such high regard that the Tacan family invites everyone with that belief system to just come out to their ranch to pray. They tie prayer flags, which are long pieces of fabric that are red, yellow, blue, or black, to the fence that encloses the buffalo. Prayers are offered to the sacred white buffalo. Some of the buffalo will separate from the herd and come over to them, look at them, and put their heads on the flags and listen to those prayers. These things are very real, as Elder Tony explained to me.

I said that I could only think that prayers would be very powerful there. Then Tony offered me a blue prayer flag so that I also could offer my prayers to the buffalo. I tied some tobacco into the prayer flag and attached it to the fence that surrounds the large area for the buffalo to roam in.

After I tied the prayer flag to the fence, the buffalo came in. Then one of the white buffalo walked up to where my prayer tie was, and I felt like the buffalo communicated with me. I felt I connected to the white buffalo. I actually felt his spirit, and when I looked into his eyes, I could tell he was looking back at me. I could feel him, and I knew he felt me too, just for a moment, but it was a moment that I will never forget.

I felt like he was telling me how grateful he was for my prayers for him and his Nation, but I also felt that he was reminding me that I was carrying his medicine. Andre had given me the glass bead so long ago that I had forgotten about it until that moment, but I now had the chance to connect to a white buffalo one on one. There were so many other buffalo all around, but this one particular white buffalo approached my prayer tie, walked up to me, and looked me in the eyes. There was a communication there, like he was telling me that he was also one of my totems. I knew then that I not only carried Bear Medicine and Eagle Medicine but also White Buffalo Medicine.

I knew that the medicine of the White Buffalo was going to walk with me in life in a good way as well. It was a Spirit Totem and a Power Totem combined into one powerful totem for me. I felt the combined energy within this one buffalo.

Buffalo are formidable and, in large numbers, intimidating. They are still wild animals, and we need to be careful. They are such powerful and amazing animals, nothing short of magnificent. When I got to go out into the field where they all were, after I fed them and watered them, I stood in the flatbed of a pickup truck as they were let into the enclosure, and this was filmed for the episode of *Spirit Talker*. These buffalo are so immensely powerful that they could literally use their head and their horns and lift the truck and flip it. One of them could have done that by itself, and there I was, standing in the open bed of the truck with a few camera guys, and over 100 buffalo were running toward us. It was very intense. It was like we were a boulder in a river and the herd was flowing all around us on either side.

It was such a spiritual moment; I felt such a connection to the buffalo, and I never even realized it was within me to feel that way. I knew that there was a message that I had to deliver through life, and I had been called to help and serve the world in so many different ways, to protect the environment, the Animal Nation, and I hoped to be doing that, beginning from that moment on.

As I continued watching the buffalo, I noticed that another white buffalo walked over to one of the prayer ties that were put on the fence and placed its head upon it. It was like it was hearing the prayers of someone else who had placed the prayer tie there. I knew that the white buffalo that leaned its head on my prayer tie heard my prayer. My prayer was for the Buffalo Nation, for the people who watched over them, for the environment, and for the world.

I knew then that the medicine of the White Buffalo was with me and that it was no accident that I had been given the glass bead containing the ashes of the white buffalo. It was no accident that we were meeting again to reaffirm and remind me that they walk with me, too, as one of my totems and that I carry their medicine with me in my heart. As my life purpose unfolds, I feel a calling to help the environment, the world, and the Animal Nation as I walk with the White Buffalo Medicine and Totems.

CHAPTER 11

♦ ♦ ♦ ♦

Ku'ku'kwes—Kesp+pit
To'tm Neya'lsit

THE OWL—MY FINAL TOTEM REVEALS ITSELF

Throughout my life, even as I was discovering my three Animal Totems, I had been having many encounters with owls as well, but I didn't know the Owl Nation would also be one of my totems that would be walking with me through life, at least not yet anyway. As I move on to this next stage of my life, I believe that one more totem will emerge, and there have been clues from Spirit that it will be the Owl Medicine. I have only ever looked at owls in awe and amazement, just because of their beauty and how gracefully they move through the air without making a sound.

Once, while I was out looking for a missing Indigenous man in New Brunswick, Canada, a white owl flew down and sat on a tree branch in front of me and other members of the search party. I felt that the missing man was trying to tell me that he had made his way home to the spirit world, and he sent me an owl as his messenger. He was in a good space in spite of the circumstances surrounding his disappearance. Nobody really knows what happened to him. He was never found.

Many times I have driven through the woods in my side-by-side, and on one occasion, I was traveling through the woods with my friend Grant when an owl perched on a branch in a tree right in front of my vehicle. I stopped and turned off my machine and walked into the woods a little bit. I noticed that when the owl took flight again, I could hear nothing, literally nothing. There was no sound from the wings, and it just made me realize how gracefully they move through the world. There is a distinct medicine that comes with the owls in that regard.

I had another very significant dream that brought the owl to me in physical life. It was, oddly enough, a dream about eagles. Knowing that the Eagle Totem is part of my Nation, in this dream, I started to have a vision that I was in the sky with other eagles. As I flew through the sky with them, I noticed that some of the eagles looked healthy and were fully mature bald eagles, and that they were each carrying a pure white tail feather in their talons. I thought that was significant because that's my Indigenous name, White Eagle Spirit Talker, so here I was, a white eagle, flying through the sky along with a few other eagles. As I looked around at hundreds of other eagles that I was surrounded by, I noticed that they seemed to be flying in pairs as mates.

They did not seem healthy or well. I became concerned for them because they were struggling to fly. There was ice accumulating on their wings. I saw that with each pair of eagles, one of them would land on the back of the other eagle and pick off the ice that had formed on its partner's feathers. They would take turns picking off the ice as they continued to fly so we could make it to our destination. I had no idea where we were headed, though.

Eventually, we landed in front of a church hall. There was a church nearby, but as all the eagles landed outside of this church, none of them wanted to go inside, even though many of them needed help. The eagles used their talons to bang on the door of the church hall instead, hoping someone would hear them and answer. Somebody did come. It was a priest from the church itself, and a request was made to him that we, the eagles, be given our own space. We said, "We feel that you have taken away who we are from us, and we need to remember who we are. We need our own sacred space to remember that."

The priest agreed to allow us to have our own space so that we could build a long building that had an opening on one end. I saw the eagles go within this great hall, along with the healthy eagles carrying white feathers, who I now know were Elders. I would say that the great hall was a representation of a longhouse. The eagles that had ice on their wings, the many hundreds of eagle couples that were there and that had been flying with me that day, were all inside this longhouse with the other Elders, and I saw the ice melting off their wings. Then I woke up.

My first thought was, *Oh, my God, this is so amazing!* I knew that dream meant something. I thought, *Who should I talk to? Who should I call?* because I wanted to speak to an Elder. I have been graced with so many Elders in my life to make connections with, so I prayed to Spirit to show me who I should reach out to. I got inspiration to call an Elder named Danny Paul.

I looked up Danny Paul's Facebook profile so I could send him a message and tell him about my dream, and when I looked at his profile picture, he was actually holding an eagle in his hands. I thought, *No wonder Spirit guided me to him. He's the perfect person I need to talk to about this.*

This all happened a little over a week before Christmas. I phoned him, and I told him about my dream, and he said,

"You know, Shawn, our people do not have our own longhouse, and I've been thinking about building one for a long time. Our Elders need a place to share our teachings, to help our people to be well and find who we are again."

Due to colonization, Indigenous people have lost their culture and their sense of who they are. This causes great suffering, not having any spiritual grounding to be well in life, spiritually and mentally, and that was represented in my dream by the eagles not being able to fly freely on their own because of the ice on their feathers. Rather than turning to the Church for help, which is where Indigenous people have been hurt in the past, we should have our own space to remember who we are and to remember the culture that we once had and to have it shared by Elders in a space like this.

I thought that what Danny Paul had in mind for a longhouse was a really good thing, and I asked Danny how I could help. He told me all he needed from me was my time. I said, "Okay, you have my time. In the spring, we'll get together." He said he already had a place picked out for the longhouse, and I was going to help build one. I wasn't intending to go there to teach. It was my intention to allow the Elders of the Mi'kmaq people in my Indigenous community to teach people who weren't balanced or well in life to find the medicine that they needed to walk through life in a good way. Some of the Eagle Medicine, I knew, was part of that spiritual guidance. I ended my phone conversation with Danny Paul, and I was looking forward to working on this project together.

On Christmas Eve I was driving to my mother-in-law's home with my wife, Michelle, for Christmas Eve dinner. As I was driving to her house, I saw a white owl perched upon a telephone wire. I had been gifted with different owl feathers in my life that I had not used, but I've always kept them. I believe that the owl feathers that I have been gifted are a clue

The Owl—My Final Totem Reveals Itself

that I will be working with Owl Medicine one day. Instead I always used Eagle Medicine in regard to smudging because I knew that the Eagle Totem already walked with me in life.

When I saw this white owl, I felt that it had a message for me. I stopped my car, and I got out and stared at the owl up on the telephone wire. I felt like the owl could see into my soul as it looked me in the eyes. It was trying to tell me that news was coming. I felt I was going to hear about something important very soon. I also sensed a kind of Elder energy when I saw it. I wondered what it could be all about.

I said to myself, "Maybe when I get home, I will call Danny Paul and ask him about what he thinks the owl means." When I got home after Christmas Eve dinner, I decided to look him up again, and I found out some very tragic news. When I went to his Facebook page, I found out from people posting condolences on his wall that he had passed away the day before I had seen the white owl, on December 23.

I thought about the dream that I had, and I felt like Danny was sending me the owl. He was an Elder, and I felt like he was giving me the message that I was still supposed to help with the longhouse project in some way in the future and that he was going to guide me with it and maybe guide the right people to me. I also realized that the owl was trying to tell me that I was going to be an Elder one day as well. I realized then that one of the Eagle Elders in the longhouse dream was Elder Danny Paul. I felt that he was gifting me the medicine of the Owl, so that when I do move into that stage of my life, I will be able to use that medicine to help people.

Right now I am 53 years old, and typically, to be an Elder in any Indigenous community, I would have to be at least 55 or older. I am not there yet. I don't want to call myself an Elder at this point in my life, and it's also not something that has been bestowed upon me yet. I feel, though, that I've already been given the Owl Medicine from Danny Paul so that when I do embrace that stage in my life, becoming an Elder, the Owl Medicine will walk through me and with me. I feel that when Elders pass away, they work with others and through others as Elders themselves.

There had been clues of the owl being one of my totems throughout my life, because they kept showing up in ways that I thought were odd, but it wasn't until Danny Paul interpreted my dream that I deepened my connection to the Owl Nation, and I felt that maybe I wasn't ready to carry that medicine yet because I'm not of age to become an Elder. In a few short years, however, I'm going to have to embrace that medicine much more. My hope is that Danny Paul will help me from the spirit world, and as I carry the Owl Medicine, he will follow me into the next stage of my life. I have yet to walk fully into the medicine of the Owl Nation, but I feel like the medicine has already been given to me for when I do get there. I have spoken to Elder Danny Paul's widow, and we have made tentative plans to build the longhouse from my dream in his memory.

Wela'lin, Daniel Joseph Paul, February 10, 1959–December 23, 2023. Thank you for your kindness and wisdom that you have shared and will continue to share with me and others from the spirit world.

Msit No'kmaq—All my relations.

CHAPTER 12

♦ ♦ ♦ ♦

Newk+l Wais+suwe'l Mpisu'nn Wije'wuksi'kl Mimajuwaqniktuk

THE FOUR ANIMAL MEDICINES THAT WALK WITH US IN LIFE

Throughout my life, there have been hints of Animal Medicine that have come to me at different times. Did I know that they were my totems? No, I didn't even really identify with my culture in the early stages of my life. It wasn't until the later stages of my life that I would identify the Animal Medicines that came to me as Spirit Totems or Power Totems. However, I feel that now that I am moving into the last stage of my life, approaching the stage of Elder, once I pass the age of 55 and I continue to walk through life in a good, spiritual way as an Indigenous person, I will walk with the Owl Medicine as well. I hope that people will look up to me in the way that they regard other Elders when I come of age as an Elder myself.

Looking back on my life now, I can see that there are four distinct animals that have come to me at different stages of my life. I firmly believe that they also come to everyone as well at the different stages of their lives. I feel that we all keep the Animal Medicines that have come to us in earlier stages.

We do not lose a previous animal's medicines as we enter different stages of life. I believe that we all have at least four Animal Medicines that come to us throughout our lifetime.

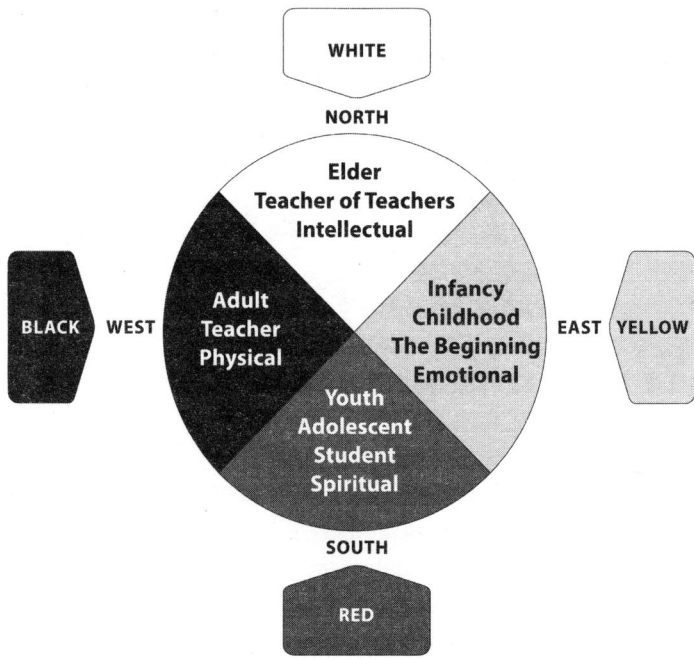

According to the Medicine Wheel, in Indigenous culture, we have four stages of life. We have Infancy, Youth, Adult, and Elder. The stages of life do not necessarily correspond to physical ages, although they may roughly correspond to them. The stages are more about the emotional, spiritual, physical, and intellectual growth of the person. These correspond to the Four Cardinal Directions and the four colors on the Medicine Wheel. East is the yellow direction, where the sun rises, and it represents our Infancy and childhood as participants, and is the beginning. South is the red direction and represents Youth and the student phase of life. It is where the deep, rich red soil is. West is the black direction, where the sun sets and the darkness comes, and it represents the Adult and teacher stage. The North direction is white, the white land, the snow and ice of the Arctic, and maybe even the white hair of the Elder phase of life, the teacher of teachers.

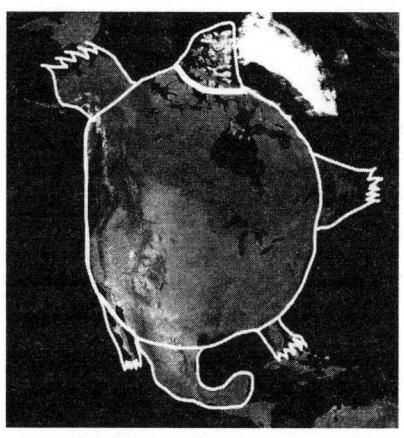

The world as our ancestors knew it was referred to as Turtle Island. Indigenous people have always referred to the Earth, but particularly North America, as Turtle Island. Now, as we see the world from a much larger perspective, we see that North America as viewed from outer space really does look like the shape of a turtle. That's why we say that we are Star People and that we had connections to Star Beings from other worlds.

I've been taught things like that from different Elders over time. Danny Paul was one of those people who shared that teaching with me. He was the one who taught me about Turtle Island, and that the Indigenous people and the Star People were our relations from other worlds. The reason we saw our continent, North America, as a giant turtle, was that we were able to visit with our Star Friends and to see the world from a different perspective. The bottom, where Mexico is narrow, is the tail of the turtle; Nova Scotia and Maine to the right is the right claw; the left claw would be Alaska; and then Northern Canada, up to the North Pole, would be the head of the turtle itself.

Now, however, we know that the world is much bigger than just North America, and we see that the colors of the wheel also represent the people of the world. It teaches us that it takes a whole wheel to make a whole world, and it's not just about Indigenous people in North America. We are all here together. We are all in one hoop of life. We are all Indigenous to somewhere.

Also, with the four stages within the Four Cardinal Directions—East, South, West, and North—there are four stages of life associated with the Medicine Wheel. As we walk in life, we will see each of these stages and the different lessons for each stage of life. I also feel that throughout my experiences in life, even though all these different animals were connected to me, they really revealed themselves at unique and specific stages that also correlated with the Medicine Wheel.

Now I understand that for each stage of life there's an Animal Medicine that walks with us all, and I think that regardless of whether we think it's uniquely Indigenous to North America or not, all of us have a deep connection to the Animal Nation from all around the world. We are all Indigenous from one place or another. What I am trying to teach here is that we all have at least four animals that walk with us through life, depending on what stage of life we are in. These animals will reveal themselves to us.

The four animals throughout our life each bring a different medicine. For myself, the Eagle brings me spiritual insight, allowing me to see things from a higher perspective, as it's a Spirit Totem Animal. The Bear represents bravery, helping me confront negative situations throughout my life with courage. The Buffalo or Bison is about respect: for others, for myself, for my culture, for people. The Owl represents wisdom, grace, and moving through life in a good way. Some Indigenous Nations may also refer to the Owl as the Night Eagle, which provides higher knowledge, insight, and illumination.

I also think it is significant that all four of my Totem Animals are white in color: my name, White Eagle—though white eagles don't exist in nature—White Polar Bear, White Buffalo, and White Owl. I feel that the medicine of the White Owl will fit into my life as I move forward into the stage of Elder. I really want to help people connect with their Animal Totems, and especially if people are over the age of 55, I would say that they already have four animals that walk with them in life, no matter where in the world they are Indigenous to. Maybe we all get clues as to what those animals are. If people read this book and are still young, maybe they are aware of some Animal Medicine that walks with them now. Maybe there is an animal that they feel a deep connection to already.

Another important teaching from my Indigenous culture is that of the Seven Directions, not to be confused with the Four Cardinal Directions of the Medicine Wheel. When we pray to the Creator to reveal to us our Totem Animals, it is important to remember all of the Directions. The Seven Directions involve those same principles as the Medicine Wheel's Four Cardinal Directions, but they also include the additional directions of Above, embodied by Father Sky and Grandfather Sun; Below, connecting us to Mother Earth; and Within, allowing us to focus inwardly on ourselves. The number seven is important to Indigenous culture and to the Mi'kmaq people. We have the Seven Directions, the Seven Sacred Grandfather Teachings, and we honor the seven generations that have come before us and the seven generations that will follow. The Seven Directions are used in our ceremonies and are an extension of the teachings within the Medicine Wheel.

I know this to be true: if we are open to it, at different stages of our life, our Animal Totems *will* reveal themselves to us. If we are stuck or not committed spiritually, they may not reveal themselves to us . . . yet. When we are moving through life in alignment with Spirit, these things will reveal themselves or may have already revealed themselves. Animal Medicine is always there, but different Animal Totems will step up, depending on which stage in life people are going through. I would encourage people to think about where they are in life, in which stage they identify themselves as being. If they are more mature, in a later stage in life, they might already be able to identify which Animal Medicines walk with them now. If not, there is a ceremonial meditation and a prayer in Chapter 14 that can help them bridge the connection.

CHAPTER 13

♦ ♦ ♦ ♦

Kepmo'ltite'wk Wais+sk Wsitqamu'k

SACRED ANIMALS AROUND THE WORLD

Recently, I had a meeting with a woman named Nubbia, who is taking my course, Spirit Talker Tribe, and she shared with me some of the medicines that are important to her and to her people from South America. She is Indigenous to Ecuador. She told me about the condor, the largest bird in the world, and the medicine that the condor brings to her and her people. It is the highest-flying bird in the world, and for that reason it is believed to be a messenger to the spirit world in the heavens. Her people also use tobacco in their ceremonies, but a bit differently than we do here. I appreciated learning from her, because I know that it's not just Indigenous people from Turtle Island, or North America, who have a deep connection to the Animal Nation. There are so many cultures across the world that also work with Animal Medicine. Even though here we do focus on the Mi'kmaq beliefs, since that is what I can share, I feel we should have a baseline of knowledge of how animals are integral to other cultures. I hope to share that with you in this chapter.

If we research the different cultures of the world and their spiritual connection to the Animal Nation, we find that they all have deep spiritual roots that intertwine with animals and are part of their spiritual beliefs. Even the way they perform their ceremonies are similar to one another. It's not just Native North America that shares these customs.

In North America we have the Native people of different Nations, like the Mi'kmaq, the Lakota, the Hopi, and many others. We all have profound connections to animal symbols that play a crucial role in our spiritual practices. Although it might not be common knowledge to many Indigenous people, even within North America, we do know something about Eagle Medicine, Bear Medicine, and so on. We have the Seven Grandfather Teachings of the seven animals that are deeply connected to our culture, which are the Wolf, the Turtle, the Bear, the Eagle, the Bison or Buffalo, the Beaver and Sabe or Bigfoot. I teach about the different medicines that they bring in regard to the Seven Grandfather Teachings in my *Wisdom of the Elders Oracle* card deck and also further on in this book. There are so many animals throughout the world, and not just the usual animals we typically think of that walk upon the Earth, but within the Animal Nation there are insects above and beneath the ground or flying in the air, birds of the sky, the fish of the sea, and so many other creatures. Every living creature has something to teach us.

The Innu on Turtle Island are still connected to the Mi'kmaq people through the Algonquin language here in North America, although they live in the Labrador and Northern Quebec region. They rely heavily on reindeer or caribou for sustenance and survival, and for clothing and food as well. I do know that they have a very deep spiritual connection in regard to all of those traditions. Innu culture often incorporates animal symbolism in their stories that their Elders share in relation to the Animal Nation.

In other regions of the world, Indigenous peoples such as the Māori of New Zealand have a rich culture and tradition of incorporating animals into their spiritual practices and mythology. Animals are often seen as spiritual guides to their people, and they act as messengers from the spiritual realms. The kiwi, the tui, the tuatara, the whale, and the shark all play important roles in Māori culture, folklore, and spirituality.

Various Indigenous peoples across Africa also have deep connections to the animal kingdom, and animals are often featured in folklore, rituals, and dances that symbolize the important qualities that animals have as spiritual messengers. It is forbidden to kill Totemic Animals, which include Cattle, the Lion, the Elephant, and the Eagle. If we observe different Indigenous groups across Africa dancing, acting according to their sacred animals, it is just amazing to see how different people interact with the medicine of the Spirit Animals themselves.

The Sámi people of Northern Europe are an Indigenous group that I have been interested in learning about lately. I watched a film called *Stolen*, based on real events, dealing with their culture as reindeer herders, and I learned that the Sámi people are Indigenous to Northern Europe. They inhabited Nordic regions of Sweden, Norway, Finland, and Russia for centuries and have a traditional animistic worldview where animals are considered spiritual beings. They have very often revered and protected the reindeer herds. They move them throughout the land itself. The reindeer hold great cultural and spiritual significance to them.

In the Swedish film *Stolen*, some people did not respect the sacredness of the reindeer, and one man in particular was just killing them, hoping to drive out the Sámi people and destroy their way of life. The herds were protected by certain Sámi families. The children were even given a reindeer to protect, and they would have a special connection to that reindeer throughout their life, marking their ears with special cuts that would identify their guardian. They even named their reindeer and had a relationship with them almost as pets.

The horrible person in *Stolen* killed a little girl's reindeer in front of her, the sacred animal and pet that she loved and whose care she was responsible for overseeing. I learned a lot about Sámi culture from this incredible film.

The Celts of Ireland, the Isle of Man, Wales, and Cornwall all shared their own beliefs about the sacredness of the trees and the tree of life, and they also incorporated animals into their beliefs and traditions as well. The Druids were the priests among the Celts, and their sacred animals included bears, horses, crows, wolves, snakes, dogs, and cats. The stag and the raven were also significant in the Irish Celtic tradition.

The Celts believed that certain abilities and characteristics of these animals could be called upon by people who might need their powers and protection in their lives. This is very similar to the traditions of North American Indigenous people.

I do have some Irish ancestry, about 30 percent. I feel a deep connection to the Druids and the Celts. I feel very drawn to Irish music and Celtic culture. I love watching movies that are related to this and have enjoyed *The Lord of the Rings*, one of my favorite movies because of the elves, the dwarves, the Celts, and the connection to the British Isles.

Shamanism is also significant to me as an Indigenous person and is found in Siberian traditions and in Indigenous cultures across North and South America. Shamanic practices around the world involve spiritual journeys in which they connect with an animal guide and gain insight, healing and guidance in a particular situation in life.

Whatever culture we hold and wherever we are from might decide which animals speak to us more, rather than animals from different parts of the world. That isn't always the case, though, because, again, even though there are many cultures, we could have a particular connection with an animal that is not even from our own nation. Some people in North America could have a deep connection to elephants or the great sea turtles of Hawaii. Maybe a past incarnation can explain our fascination with animals from different countries and continents around the world.

Another culture that I feel very strongly connected to is that of ancient Egypt. It is not because of my genetics, but it is related to a past-life memory. I know that I've lived a past life in Egypt. I was a sun god worshipper, a priest in a temple near Luxor, that was connected to the sun god Ra. I am really attracted to the whole culture. In Egypt, they have a very deep cultural connection to animals as well, and they played significant roles in their daily lives and belief systems.

Some animals were even mummified, a fact that I discovered when I went to Le Louvre in Paris, France. I was in France exploring some of my genealogy and family history. I was really surprised to see mummified cats on display. Cats were sacred in ancient Egypt. They had been mummified and buried with their owners. The ancient Egyptians wanted to bring their pets into the afterlife with them, which reflected their strong belief in the afterlife. There were also other sacred animals that were associated with the temples, and they would be mummified and buried in the tombs too. Although I love my own cat, I'm not sure she would want to be buried with me. She doesn't seem to like me very much sometimes, except when she's in a particularly good mood!

In the Hindu belief system, animals hold much religious and symbolic significance. For instance, the cow is considered sacred. It represents nonviolence and motherhood. The elephant-headed god Ganesh is revered as a remover of obstacles. They also believe that every being has a divine soul, and nonviolence is integral to their religion. Hindus cherish the intrinsic connection between the Human Nation and the Animal Nation.

Last but not least, the Tibetan Buddhists have beliefs about animals as protectors as well, such as the snow lion, the Garuda, the tiger, and the dragon, which are the four guardian animals that help people through different phases of life. They are featured in religious art and rituals of the Tibetan people. Also, birds are seen as totems that help with the practice of meditation. The Yeti, also known as the Abominable Snowman, is a mythical creature revered as a protector of the wilderness. The wind horse carries prayers to the gods. They are often seen on prayer flags.

Long before contact with North America and our Indigenous culture, these people from all around the world held similar beliefs about the crossover connection between animals and humans in their spirituality, even though we haven't interacted throughout the ages in different parts of the world. There is something innate within us, in all our genetics, that is deeply connected to the Animal Nation despite the culture, color of our skin, or wherever we are from in the world, in every area of the world, as we are all Indigenous to one part of the world or another. This shows that there is a connection between all of us in the Animal and Human Nations.

The ancient Greeks believed in their gods, and each of them had a connection to an animal that they would rule over in the natural world. Zeus, the greatest of the gods, had the eagle, representing courage, valor, and respect, which he would use to look over the wider world as the king of the gods. Before current day major world religions suppressed these belief systems, when humans were free-thinking people, we were able to incorporate the Animal Nation into our Human

Nation and spirituality. It's been lost, and it is time for us to remember that connection and bring it back to us.

My perspective is that no matter what culture or race we are from, we are all Indigenous to somewhere. I feel that because we didn't have angels, which came predominantly from the Judeo-Christian tradition, we had animals. The attributes and the personalities that we associate with the Archangels Michael, Raphael, Gabriel, and Uriel have been given to different Animal Nations, depending on where people were in the world. In North America, it is predominantly the Seven Grandfather Teachings of those animals that exist for us, but in Peru, there are three animals—the condor, the puma, and the snake—that they see as following them on a journey through life.

Animals have meaning and importance to each culture and there is none that is greater or better than another. I feel that whatever speaks to us, and whatever culture that is, or even if we can identify with several cultures, as I do—with Indigenous, Celtic, and Egyptian cultural beliefs—we should draw from all of them, and they are all part of our faith and spirituality. If I can do this, we can all do this. We are all from the Human Nation and we are all deeply connected to the Animal Nation.

CHAPTER 14

♦ ♦ ♦ ♦

Weji Nenujik Wais+se'k To'tmk

IDENTIFYING AND WORKING WITH OUR ANIMAL TOTEMS

By this point, you may be wondering, "What's my Animal Totem?" You may already have a really good indication about one, two, or maybe all of the Animal Totems that are walking with you in life.

If you're not there yet, at the end of this chapter there are a few helpful exercises: a prayer, a ceremonial meditation, and a questionnaire that can help you to connect to the Animal Totems that you already know you have or to reveal the ones that you are not yet aware of.

You might get one totem, or you might get them all. Either way, it is important that we work with the medicine that is being given to us, trust it, and ask for validation in some form or another.

A friend of mine named Suzan felt that she might have Turtle Medicine, but she wasn't entirely sure which Animal Totem was walking with her through her Elder phase of life. She had clues of some Spirit Animals through dreams and actual sightings of animals all her life, but she wasn't sure which Spirit Totem walked with her in her current phase of life. Since childhood, she had been gifted turtles in the form of jewelry and had given some to her own children as toys or pendants, and suddenly these turtles were turning up and catching her attention.

After making a sacred fire in her backyard fire pit and burning some sage and cedar, as well as some firewood, she prayed to her spirit guides to show her which Animal Totem walked with her in her Elder stage of life. Later that day, she cleaned under her fridge and stove, and she found a fridge magnet in the form of a sea turtle! Surprised but still unconvinced, she asked for more validation.

She then came across an article in the news about a former teacher and, looking at the photos of his apartment, counted at least 30 turtles among his art collection! Then while checking Facebook, the first friend suggestion she saw had a profile picture of a baby sea turtle making its way into the ocean. By then it was clear that the Turtle was emerging as her Spirit Totem Animal that would lend her its medicine to walk with her, in this case very slowly like a turtle, through the rest of her life! Spirit can validate which Animal Medicine we are meant to carry in many different ways, as long as we remain open to receiving it.

If we have uncertainty regarding it, we shouldn't worry about it. After all, it's taken years for my Animal Totems to reveal themselves to me! I didn't embrace my culture until my late 30s, so I didn't even know who I was as an Indigenous person until then. I feel like our Spirit Animals, which include at least two Spirit Totem Animals and two Power Totem Animals, all four of them, have always been with us, whether we have been aware of them or not.

A Spirit Totem Animal will help guide you spiritually, so that you can approach life utilizing many aspects of their sacred medicines. A Power Totem Animal offers spiritual medicines that you call upon for protection when facing life's most difficult trials, tribulations, and struggles.

They came into this life with us. They have been there all along, but we might not have been aware of them. If we have a connection with our totems already, that is amazing, or maybe we have had a connection to one or two, and we would like to know the other ones as well.

Some people might not be in that stage of life right now and still have those totems to look forward to in the future. They may only know of three, and that's okay. Maybe when we come closer to the Elder stage of life, like I am currently, that medicine will reveal itself more clearly then. When it is revealed, though, we will know without a doubt.

The way my Animal Totems have been revealed to me in my life was through speaking to the Animal Nation in ceremonies, prayers, and meditation. My totems were revealed to me, but not all of them appeared to me until I got close to that phase in my life, whether it was the Bear Medicine of my Youth, the Eagle Medicine and the White Buffalo Medicine of my Adult phase, or now the Owl Medicine emerging as I get closer to the Elder phase. The same is probably true for all of us. They are with us, but reveal themselves depending on what stage of life we are currently in.

I'm assuming that most people who are reading this book are in the Adult phase according to the Medicine Wheel. The Infancy and Youth stages are complete. Most people would already have three Animal Totems, and it is possible to deep dive to discover which animals are walking with them. If the Elder years have been reached, then maybe they are hoping for all four totems to be revealed.

I would encourage people to be patient yet persistent, remembering to make an offering of some sort, too, in relation to their request to the Animal Nation. Through their ceremony, they can offer some type of spiritual medicine, like cedar or sage or even a crystal. In Indigenous culture, we have a reciprocal principle that we follow, where we give something to get something. It's kind of like that when we go to the store. We give money to get something. We give to the Animal Nation spiritually. We give some spiritual medicine. Whatever culture people embrace in life, and there are many cultures in the world, they should try to find whatever resonates with that culture and way of life, and use that medicine.

I feel that it is really important in life that when we utilize spiritual medicines for an offering, to have our prayerful words heard, or our ceremonial words heard, the medicine we offer be gifted to us in some fashion from a family member or a close friend. We can even ask someone to gift us some medicine that aligns with our culture in particular from wherever we are in the world. Maybe we can make a request to Spirit for a family member or a close friend to gift us some of that medicine so that when we do the ceremony at the end of this chapter, we all have an offering to give.

Some examples of cultural spiritual medicine that we can burn might be, if we are Hindu, incense; if we are Christian it could be frankincense or myrrh; or if we are Indigenous it could be sage or tobacco or cedar or sweetgrass; if we are from South America we could use tobacco that is used in their religious ceremonies; or palo santo, meaning "holy wood," if we are from Mexico, Peru, or Ecuador.

Perhaps more importantly than where we are from genetically or culturally, if we do not resonate with that culture for whatever reason, we should learn about spiritual practices and customs that we do connect to and are drawn to for our spiritual good—but be careful that this learning does not turn into appropriation. Try to learn about other cultures from authorized sources, and handle customs and rituals with the utmost respect. A past-life connection to a specific or even several cultures could determine which customs we are most attracted to. Regardless, the important thing to remember is our intention. The power of our intention in our prayers and our words to Spirit make the most impact in connecting to our Totem Animals.

When we make an offering, when we say our ceremonial words, we offer this gift wholeheartedly, asking for our words to be heard and our request for our Totem Animal to come to us. Then when we do get an animal that comes to us, maybe just one at first, we may have to be persistent in asking for the rest of them to be revealed. There may be more still to come after doing the ceremony a few times and doing the meditation many times. We should not give up. We should keep trying and searching, and then when one does come, just like the friend who had the turtle showing up, it may reveal itself in a very synchronistic and very cool way to confirm that yes, we carry that Animal Medicine.

When different animals reveal themselves to us, even though there are four Totem Animals that come to us at different stages of life, we should remember that there are two that are Spirit Totem Animals and two that are Power Totem Animals. We have to keep in mind which of those Totem Animals they might be or even whether they could be both Spirit and Power Totems, such as the White Buffalo is for me.

For myself, the strength of different Animal Medicines that have come to me has been from the White Buffalo and the Bear. They are definitely Power Totem Animals that have kept me safe with their strength. They are super powerful animals, great protectors. The Eagle and the Owl are more Spirit medicine to me and are my Spirit Totem Animals. Being from the sky and closer to the higher realms, they lend me their wisdom and compassion. I also feel, though, that the

White Buffalo Medicine lends its wisdom to me on occasion as a Spirit Totem.

The Eagle or the Owl might represent a Power Totem to someone else, depending on what aspects of those animals they need in their life. Maybe when going through a tough situation, they need the speed and the clear sight of the Eagle or the stealth and the patience of the Owl. The Bear might represent the nurturing aspect of parenthood and could be a Spirit Totem to some people. The Bison is a herd animal, and they gather around their young in groups to protect them, forming a community, and in that way they may lend their Animal Medicine as Spirit Totems to others. It all depends on how our own personalities and spirits relate to them.

Whatever resonates with us best is very important in considering which totem is a Spirit Totem or a Power Totem Animal. Just because my Power Totems represent strength and protection, it doesn't mean that for another person; it could be the reverse. Only we can tell, after meditation and contemplation, which Animal Medicine our Totem Animals represent in our life and how we can use their strengths to help us. What feels right in regard to what we feel is our power and what we feel is our sacred spirit medicine in relation to the animal attributes will help us tell the difference between the two.

If you have my card deck, *Wisdom of the Elders Oracle,* you can use the cards to help clarify which of the Seven Grandfather Teachings are appearing in our life. For example, after dreaming of an animal, we might then choose Power Totem Animal from the oracle cards. After prayerful consideration, doing some research into the benefits of that Animal Medicine, we might come to the conclusion that it is true that the totem is one of our Power Totem Animals. Someone else might choose Bear or Beaver or Turtle from the cards and then the Spirit Totem card, for example. Spirit will use whatever tools we have at our disposal to get the message through to us about who walks with us in life.

I would say that we have to listen to our heart. What is it that we feel in relation to the animal that has revealed itself to us? Is it strength, protection to keep us safe, in which case it would be a Power Totem? If it is wisdom, understanding and drawing a spiritual lesson from it, it would be a Spirit Totem. One helps us go through a situation and the other helps us gain wisdom from the lessons learned in that situation. When we are going through something, it is best to call upon our Power Totem; and then on the other side of it, trying to understand why we went through it, we would call upon our Spirit Totem to ask for the wisdom gained from it.

Once our Animal Totems reveal themselves to us, we must remember to include them in all that we do. In our prayers to our spirit guides, angels, and ancestors we should also include our Spirit Totem Animals. They are here to help us through our journey in this life, and if we speak to them from the heart and request to know which animals are connected to us, they will give us signs to let us know who they are.

They will provide us with additional spiritual support to call upon in life and during moments of prayer and reflection. They impart to us their strength and their wisdom. Remember that they are always walking with us along this path and are guiding and protecting us along our journey in this life.

A Prayer to Connect to Your Spirit Animal Totems

Great Spirit,
Creator of all life,
I humbly call upon the wisdom of the Animal Nation.
Guide me to the Spirit Animal Totems that are meant to walk with me on my sacred journey,
To teach me, to protect me, and to inspire me.

I open my heart and my spirit to the energy of this sacred bond.
I will honor their wisdom with respect and gratitude.
I will listen to the messages they bring.
I will embody the qualities they wish to awaken within me.
Spirit Animals, guardians, and sacred guides,
I am ready to receive your medicine and divine guidance.
Show me the path I must walk,
And grant me the strength and courage to walk it with purpose.

At every stage of life may you make yourself clearly known to me.
May your spiritual medicines and powerful traits embody my spirit.
May our connection grow strong and true,
And may I walk in this life with your wisdom and spirit by my side.

Thank you for your presence
And for the spiritual strength and wisdom you bring.
With humility and gratitude, I honor you in the sacred hoop of life.

Msit No'kmaq—All my relations.

Spirit Totem Animal Meditation

Find a quiet and comfortable place where you won't be disturbed. Use items like sage, cedar, palo santo, frankincense, lavender, blessed water, or another sacred medicine that you are in alignment with to cleanse yourself and your space.

Use the smoke of this smudging medicine or self-blessed water or crystal as an offering to the spirit world.

If you have a drum, a rattle, or a recording of natural sounds, like the forest, a river, or birds, use that too.

Have a journal handy to record insights after the meditation.

Center yourself: Sit comfortably, either on the ground or in a chair with your feet firmly upon Mother Earth, and take a few deep breaths.

Begin by visualizing roots growing from your body deep into Mother Earth.

Feel the energy of Mother Earth supporting you, anchoring you, and connecting you to all living things.

Acknowledge the Seven Directions: East, South, West, North, Above (Father Sky and Grandfather Sun), Below (Mother Earth), and Within (Your Spirit and Heart Sacred Fire).

You can say a simple prayer:

Spirits of the East, bring clarity.
Spirits of the South, bring creativity.
Spirits of the West, bring transformation.
Spirits of the North, bring wisdom.
Sky above, Earth below, Spirit within, guide me on this journey.

Close your eyes and imagine walking through a serene, natural setting—a forest, desert, mountain, ocean, or any place that feels sacred to you.

Notice the details: the scent of the air, the texture of the ground, the sounds around you.

As you walk, set an intention: "I am open to meeting my Spirit Totem Animal."

Visualize a clearing in your path. In this space, your Spirit Totem Animal will appear.

Observe patiently. It might approach you directly or show itself subtly as a shadow, a sound, or a sensation.

Just sit in this space in contemplative meditation until your Spirit Totem Animal reveals itself to you.

When the Animal appears, greet it with respect. Ask:
- "What message or guidance do you have for me?"
- "How can I honor your spiritual wisdom?"

Listen closely to its response, which might come in words, images, feelings, or symbols.

Thank the Animal for its guidance and presence. Offer your prepared gift symbolically in the meditation by imagining placing it in the space.

Slowly retrace your steps, leaving the sacred space. Imagine returning through the natural setting and feeling grounded in your body.

Take a few deep breaths and open your eyes when ready.

Write down your experience in your journal. Include:
- The Spirit Animal you encountered
- Any messages, emotions, or symbols you received
- Thoughts on how this guidance applies to your life

Offer gratitude to the Seven Directions: the Eastern direction where the sun rises, South, West, North, the ground below/Mother Earth, the Sky above you/Grandfather Sun, and your Heart Sacred Fire and Spirit within.

If possible, leave a small physical offering in nature to honor your Spirit Totem Animal and the sacred connection.

How Do You Know Who Your Totem Animals Are?

- Did you have a favorite animal as a child?
- What was it about this animal that you admired?
- Is it the same animal now that you have as a grown-up, or is it a different animal?

- Do you keep seeing a particular animal when you are out in the world, whether at work or at home watching television or while on social media?
- Look for synchronicities. When you are out, do you see something that represents an animal continuously? Pay attention to everything from storefront signs to designs on clothing.
- Do you remember a dream about a specific animal? What happened between you and that animal?
- Do you admire a particular animal for its abilities, for example the cleverness of the fox, the swiftness of the cheetah, the music of the grasshopper, the resourcefulness of the bumblebee?
- Do you have consistent encounters with certain animals who show up out in nature?
- Do you have any collections of certain animals that you are fascinated by?
- Do an animal's traits resonate with your strengths or personality?
- Do you have a deep sense of knowing or recognition about an animal?

You can also seek help in your search: Use oracle cards or a pendulum, consult with a spiritual guide, or go on a Shamanic journey to identify your animal.

When you have an idea of who your Animal Totems are, call upon them to give you strength, wisdom and guidance in your daily life. Be sure to research them in as much depth as you can to discover their specific qualities and spiritual medicines. Journal about these animals that come to you, and explore why and how they are significant to you.

Ta'n tel Kepme'kl Luikn+kewe'l Kina'masuti'l

THE IMPORTANCE OF THE SEVEN GRANDFATHER TEACHINGS IN INDIGENOUS CULTURE

◆ ◆ ◆ ◆

Over the next seven chapters, I will focus on the Seven Grandfather Teachings in Indigenous culture. Indigenous communities in North America in particular are deeply connected to the seven animals in the Grandfather Teachings: Wolf, Turtle, Bear, Eagle, Bison and Buffalo, Beaver, and Sabe or Bigfoot. We have chosen these animals and their emanations or personalities based on how they are connected to particular medicines. By medicines, we mean the spiritual benefits that they offer us. The Grandfather Teachings are about how we can walk through life in a good way. By embodying different teachings through these different animals, we can approach life in a good way. That's why I have chosen to focus on these animals in particular. There are so many animals in the world that I could choose from, but I think it is important to teach about the Seven Grandfather Teachings of Indigenous people on Turtle Island. I don't want to just choose my own personal Totem Animals to give as examples, either. I want to write about the other animals that give particular medicines as well to show how the personas of these animals in the Animal Nation guide us through life. Even if we do not carry the medicines of these Totem Animals, we can still call upon them to help us through our journey in life.

CHAPTER 15

♦ ♦ ♦ ♦

Wanqwajite'teken—Paqtesm
HUMILITY—THE WOLF

The Wolf Medicine, which is Humility, is the first Grandfather Teaching, although it isn't medicine that I particularly carry. I have never had a connection with this animal other than at a wildlife park in Nova Scotia. I have never seen a wolf elsewhere, and I've never dreamed of a wolf, so I was very inspired to reach out to my Spirit Talker Tribe students. I felt that there must be people out there who have had experiences with the Wolf in spiritual and maybe personal encounters that would be medicine that was brought to them and which they could share.

My students Aaron and Laura both have had dreams of walking with wolves or running through fields with wolves, sometimes on two feet as humans and then on all fours as wolves. These are very powerful symbols of both running free in life, following our own instincts and intuition while at the same time having a wolf pack or community to support us.

Laura had another dream of a wolf, a "wee black baby pup" with its mother, a big black wolf. The wolves were chased away by a dog in her dream. She took this to mean that she should not be afraid to take on what seems bigger, stronger, tougher in her life and to stand up to her truth. All dogs are connected to the Wolf Nation and can also teach us Wolf Medicine, as they are ancestors.

On another occasion, Laura lit a sacred fire and prayed to her ancestors for her daughter's spiritual safety and protection and for a sign that all would go well for her. She specifically asked for two wolves to come to her in real life. That is exactly what she saw on her way home, two black wolves! That was some very powerful medicine!

Laura's story reminds me of the Cherokee folklore about the two wolves. This wisdom is traditionally passed down from an Elder to a young person who is experiencing an inner conflict. The story goes as such: There is a battle between two wolves within every person. One wolf represents good, good choices and right action in alignment with the Wolf Medicine, and the other represents evil or darkness or the wrong path. The young person asks the Elder which wolf will win this battle. The Elder replies, "The one that you feed." We can all feed good things in our life, and we can also feed our limiting beliefs. Whatever we give power to is the wolf that you feed within your own life. We are all creators of our destiny, and we can choose to feed positivity or negativity to determine the outcome of certain situations. We need to choose wisely and thoughtfully which wolf we feed.

The medicine that is particularly strong with the wolf, I feel, is their intelligence. They are highly intelligent, so when we need to approach a specific situation in life where we need to draw upon intelligence, deep connection, and even follow our instincts in relation to a particular situation, we should call upon Wolf Medicine because wolves are very good at those things. They are very courageous, and they are also very resilient. I feel like they carry a lot of wisdom and insight and they have a profound community connection. Within the community, there is a call for someone to step up to be the Alpha, the leader of a group.

If there is disorganization in a community somewhere and we feel the calling, particularly to lead the group in some way, the Wolf Medicine is something that we are more in alignment with. We have to be adaptable, and sometimes other people may need to lead, but Wolf Medicine is very determined and very strong because, through their instincts, wolves know that they have to lead the group. As the Alpha gets weaker within the group, the next part of the Wolf Nation will step up to take on that role. Even if within the Wolf Nation they are not in a leadership role, they are always ready or able to step up into that role if need be. Leadership is instinctually within every one of them.

It is not something that is done alone, either. There are hardly any lone wolves or outcasts. They have a deep community connection within the pack that they work with as well as a deep inner wisdom and a call for leadership within the community, to bring clarity, to bring guidance, to bring support, to help each other face different adversities and situations in life. Wolf Medicine is really good for that.

Another Spirit Talker Tribe student named Lana shared her experience with Wolf Medicine, and it illustrates this medicine in an amazing way. A few years ago, she found herself alone as a single mother with four sons to raise. She was "in great need of security, belonging, and a tribe," she writes. She had a very vivid dream one night of a wolf pack. "Their beautiful eyes looked right into my soul. At first, I was afraid, and then I realized they were surrounding my children and me and guiding us into their den. The feeling was one of adoption, that we were being adopted and included into their family." After that dream, she writes that she felt safe and that she had a Spirit Tribe that welcomed her family. She felt she belonged after that.

Wolf medicine, according to the Seven Grandfather Teachings that I wrote about in my *Wisdom of the Elders Oracle* card deck, is about Humility. Humility teaches us that we are all equal, no one is better than another, and the pack must operate as one. Each member must understand its role within the group. The same is true for us when we need help. It takes humility to sincerely ask for help. The Wolf is our greatest teacher. It bows its head while in the presence of others and will not take food until all members of the pack have received a share. This shows a great respect for the community. In order for a community to run smoothly, each member must fulfill their role and contribute to the well-being of all. In this way, the Wolf Spirit Totem works within our life, offering us its wisdom and peacefully living within a community.

As a Power Totem, wolves cannot be easily domesticated and in that way, they march to the beat of their own drum, so to speak. They represent freedom and living life according to their instincts. They have to live like wolves. It comes down to taking a leadership role and having belief in ourselves and stepping into that role because it is instinctually within us to do that, to take control of situations when sometimes we feel they are out of control. Running with wolves in dreams represents aligning with our people in life, finding our tribe. When we find our people, it is important to find those who are in alignment with us.

Humility—The Wolf

Prayer of the Humble Wolf

Great Spirit.
Creator of all life, seen and unseen,
I come before You with a heart seeking humility
Teach me, like the wolf,

To walk gently upon the Earth,
To honor the balance of nature,
And to embrace my role within the pack of life.

Grant me the wisdom of the wolf,
Who knows when to lead and when to follow,
Who finds strength in unity yet respects solitude.

May I learn from its quiet endurance,
From its howl that echoes through the mountains,

Calling not for pride but for connection.
Humble my spirit, Creator,
So that I may tread lightly on the path You set before me,
Without arrogance but with purpose and gratitude.

Let me see through the eyes of the wolf,
Keen and watchful,
Aware of the beauty and fragility of this world.

Guide me to serve others with loyalty and love,
To protect what is sacred,
And to approach each moment with humility,
Knowing I am but one part of Your vast creation.
In the stillness of the forest,

In the moonlight's gentle glow,
Let my soul sing in harmony with Yours,
As the wolf howls to all Spirits.

Msit No'kmaq—All my relations.

◆ ◆ ◆ ◆

CHAPTER 16

♦ ♦ ♦ ♦

Wanqwajite'teken—Paqtesm
TRUTH—THE TURTLE

The turtle is seen as Truth in Indigenous culture. We call North America Turtle Island, and we all live on the back of the turtle. It was here at the creation of the world. It is one of the oldest animals on our planet and has incredible longevity. It carries all seven of the Grandfather Teachings, which are love, wisdom, respect, bravery, honesty, humility, and truth. It also carries all 13 full moons on its shell and 28 markings around the edge of its shell, representing a woman's 13 moon cycles within a year. Turtles walk around with a calendar on their backs. There must be something about timing, because they've been here as one of the longest-living animals on the Earth. They are here to teach us about being good caretakers of our time. They remind us of the time that we go with in life.

People who carry Turtle Medicine share certain characteristics of the turtle. The Turtle is very hard and can be self-protective, and in this way it can be a Power Totem: very hard when it turns its back on someone, but it also has a very soft underbelly. People carrying Turtle Medicine can call upon the strength of their shell to shield them from life's struggles, acting as a protective barrier against negative situations in life. Sometimes when Turtle people know that they are among people who they can trust, they open up to those people. When they have a friend, they can open up to that friend; otherwise, they tend to be very cautious.

They embody Spirit Totem medicine in some regard as well. Their home is where they go, and they can live anywhere. They may have certain places where they like to be, and if they had to travel long distances they could, and they take their home with them. Wherever they are is where they feel at home. They are also very family oriented.

I have a condo in Aruba, where there are spaces that are set up for turtles to go and lay their eggs. When the eggs are hatching, everybody wants to go out and see them because it is so amazing. The turtles lay many eggs on the beach, where there are many birds that the eggs must be protected from.

When the baby turtles do get out into the ocean, it is a fish-eat-fish world out there, with sharks and other predators trying to eat them all the time. They have to stay close to shore where it is safe, and they know where the sandy spots are where the sharks don't go. They have this wisdom, which is innate, spiritual wisdom, making sure that they are safe. Their innate wisdom helps them make decisions about where they are so that they can avoid being in predicaments where they would be vulnerable. They have to be put in spaces where they feel safe.

Turtle people are very cautious about where they do live or where they do go, the people they do hang around with. They are also very adaptable, like turtles, who can go back and forth between the sea and the shore, and in that way they can stay safe. People who have Turtle Medicine can move out of a situation; even though they can see a problem, they can step outside of it, just like the turtle can move outside of water and back onto land. They can take themselves out of dangerous situations if need be.

Baby turtles are at their most vulnerable on the beach, but when they go out to sea, they are on their own from a very young stage, much like Turtle people, who tend not to have the best parental figures growing up. They feel that they have to look out for themselves in many ways.

Turtles are a lot stronger than they look, and this is part of their power. I have swum with the turtles in Hawaii, and they are very amazing, graceful animals. Just being with them is like having a spiritual experience. It is just the same with people who carry Turtle Medicine. When others come into contact with them, they find that they like to be around them because they have a Zen energy about them, a kindness about them, a gentleness, a certain grace when they go through things in life. Even though it might be a struggle for the Turtle people, we see them as handling things very well and very gracefully, just like turtles move through the water, with an elegance, a softness, a gentleness, a kindness, a compassion for other living things.

When I was in the water swimming with them, that is what I experienced. It was amazing. Actually, every time I go to a tropical destination, if I find out there are turtles in that area, I try to spend time with them. I try to swim with them just to be among them. I don't think about the sharks that might come and eat me. I think more about just spending time with the turtles because I enjoy their presence, their medicine, their energy, and what they embody spiritually.

Turtles have lived on Earth for millions of years. If we look at the human world, we've evolved through time, but turtles have kept their reptilian aspect that existed long before humanity. This is a testament to their strength and their determination to overcome things in the long term that helps them get through so much over time, and they do it with such grace. The longevity of a turtle is immense as well because I feel like it has a lot to do with the way they react to the world.

Typically, if someone has Turtle Medicine, it's really good medicine to have because they are going to have a very long life. That doesn't mean that they are not going to endure struggles, but they have a way of moving outside of situations, moving like a turtle on land if they need to, moving back into the water when they feel it is safe, and if Turtle people had to pick up and go from one space to another, one culture to another, one family to another if they had to, they would.

I think turtles are amazing spiritual teachers, showing us how we can interact and engage with the world. Their power is their resilience. Their strength is their shell. They are a lot stronger than they appear because they are such gentle animals, and Turtle people are very gentle, kind, and compassionate, so people may forget how powerful they are as well. If we could all draw a lot of those elements to us, we could learn a lot from them.

Also, turtles teach us Truth, because that's the aspect of the Seven Grandfather Teachings that they embody. All the teachings work together as a whole within Turtle Medicine. Turtle teaches us to be truthful with ourselves in order to embrace all the Grandfather Teachings. To truly understand and express love, one must know wisdom, respect, bravery, honesty, humility, and truth. It is by embracing all Seven Grandfather Teachings that we can truly live a good and healthy life.

The turtle is very deeply connected to Grandmother Moon and Mother Earth as well. It was here during the creation of the Earth so that the teachings would never be lost or forgotten. Turtle is there to remind us of our connection to Grandfather Sun and the cycles of the moon itself, carrying all 13 full moon cycles on its shell. Turtles are one of the oldest animals on our planet and live their life in a slow and deliberate manner. Turtles understand the importance of both the journey and the destination.

Because of the turtle's longevity, their power is that they always have time on their side. They can endure whatever they are going through, so their longevity is a strength that they carry, a spiritual medicine that enables them to move out of a situation that does not serve their highest good. After they have gone through it, they go back to their natural state of being, finding their space in life. The spiritual medicine that they carry, their wisdom, comes through their longevity. They have the grace of understanding all Seven Grandfather Teachings and embody them so that they will actually walk through life as Truth.

A Prayer for Truth, Time, and the Turtle's Wisdom

Great Spirit,
Keeper of truth and guardian of time,
I come before you with a humble heart,
Seeking the wisdom of the turtle,
The gentle keeper of time, patience, and steadfastness.

Teach me, Great Spirit, to carry truth upon my back,
As the turtle carries its shell—
Not as a burden but as a sanctuary,
A place where honesty dwells and peace resides.

Help me to walk slowly but surely,
Embracing the journey over the destination,
For in each moment lies a lesson,
And in every step, a truth revealed.

May I honor time as the turtle does,
Unhurried and deliberate,
Trusting that all things unfold as they should,
In the rhythm of Your divine plan.

Allow me to shed all things that do not serve my journey,
Choosing instead the enduring path of integrity.
May I find strength in stillness,
And courage in the quiet persistence of faith.

Great Spirit of Time and Truth,
Guide me to see with clarity,
To move with purpose,
And to live with the quiet wisdom of the turtle.

In patience, in truth, and unconditional love.
Msit No'kmaq—All my relations.

CHAPTER 17

♦ ♦ ♦ ♦

Melkita'mkewey—Muin

BRAVERY—THE BEAR

The third aspect of the Seven Grandfather Teachings is the Bear, representing bravery. I have shared throughout this book many different bear stories, like facing a bear when I was running in the adventure race in British Columbia. I obviously had no choice then but to be brave. I could either whimper and cower or really stand up to the bear and let it know I was there, facing my biggest fear. There have been many times in my life when I've had to use Bear Medicine.

To face change and adversity in life, we have to be brave. Oftentimes, we are faced with hard situations that we just don't expect. There are some good people out there who are going to come into our life to fight for us when we need them, and I feel like Bear Medicine guides them to me. When we go through struggles in life, it's important to remember that we have Power Animal Totems or Spirit Animal Totems. The strength, the bravery, and the courage of the Bear has helped me in my life's toughest situations. Just because I am a spiritual person and have spiritual teaching doesn't mean that I don't face adversity. I have faced difficult situations throughout my life, and I think it's important to know that every person will. Nobody gets a free pass. The essential thing is how we face it and who faces it with us.

So, calling upon our Animal Totems, both Spirit and Power, with the energy that they carry within the Seven Grandfather Teachings, is very important. Remembering that they are there will help us face life's challenging situations. For myself, I know that I couldn't have made it through without their help. Standing up for what is right and fearlessly defending our truth like a mother bear defending her cubs is what Bear Medicine represents, and I have gratitude for the Bear Medicine that walks with me through life.

Even if the Bear is not one of our Totem Animals, we can still call upon Bear Medicine to help us when, for example, protecting our children, in much the same way we might also call upon Archangel Michael for courage. Bears have fearless hearts, and bravery is the gift that the Bear provides to us. Although these animals are gentle by nature, they will fight to the death if they need to protect their young. The ferociousness of the mother bear epitomizes the teaching of bravery.

Bear's courageousness teaches us to have mental and moral strength to overcome the fears that prevent us from fully engaging in this specific sacred Grandfather Teaching. It is a challenge that must be faced with the same level of strength and intensity as a mother bear protecting her cub. Bear shows us that we should face our challenges. That is the Bear Medicine. When we feel like we are avoiding a situation in life, we have to step into it head-on. Dr. Wayne Dyer famously said, "What you resist will persist." We cannot avoid certain situations in life that are meant to be teaching us great lessons. If we think we can avoid facing adversity, it will turn up in another area or at another time in our lives.

In many traditional native cultures, Bear Medicine also represents healing, self-reliance, the power of introspection, and finding the answers and remedies within oneself. There have been many times in my life when I have had to incorporate Bear Medicine and step out into the unknown. As a young man, the first time was when I had just finished high school: I was living at home with my mom, and my relationship with my girlfriend ended when she moved away and joined the military. I decided to explore life and figure out who I was meant to be, so I moved from Nova Scotia to Newfoundland to live with my Mi'kmaq grandmother, Margaret. While there, I worked for a year as a cod fisherman with my uncle Sam. The harsh weather on the Atlantic Ocean was quite cold and unforgiving, but I loved being outdoors and I loved fishing. It was a great way of life, but unfortunately, I didn't make enough money to invest in anything. I could see that the cod industry was dying, along with a lot of other industries related to fishing, so I didn't see a great future for me there.

In this self-discovery period, I needed to figure out how I was going to provide for myself in life. I knew I couldn't stay in Newfoundland, and there were just no opportunities for me back in Nova Scotia either. Calgary, however, seemed like a booming space and place, and I did have some aunts who lived there. So, I decided to set out on a journey of healing, of learning to love myself, becoming more self-reliant, and finding some of my own inner strength so that I could step up in life and be the man that I was hoping to become. It took a tremendous amount of bravery to leave the comfort of living at home and all of the Maritimes behind.

When I moved out to Calgary, I got a job at Hayworth, a company that made office furniture. I worked my way up there for 15 years, until I was making a fairly good wage for that time. While I was happy, I realized I wasn't going to be able to stay there indefinitely when they began laying people off, so I left for a new career with Canada Post.

Shortly thereafter I felt a calling to move back home to Nova Scotia and to come full circle in my life. But I was no longer a young man looking for a job and direction. Now, as a married man with two teenage daughters, I urgently felt the importance of being able to support myself and my family. I also knew it would be a big ask to make of my family. My wife was from British Columbia while both my girls were born here in Alberta, and they'd need to leave everything they knew for the opposite coast of Canada. If things didn't work out, I would be putting us all in a bad spot. It required a lot of bravery to make the decision and believe that I could do it.

Initially, I moved back to Nova Scotia by myself, and it felt like a repeating pattern: I had to be self-reliant, to make a new life on my own once again, buying a new home and getting everything ready for my wife and children to join me. I wanted everything to be just right for us. They did join me eventually, but unfortunately a divorce also followed shortly afterward. Once again, I found myself on a healing journey of strength, bravery, and self-reliance.

In order to step out into the world as the person I am today, a professional spirit talker and psychic medium, I had to find balance, wellness, and inner strength. I had to be brave enough to find my passion, to express myself in life, and create a life based on Bear Medicine. There have been so many times when I've had to go through healing, find my inner strength, and become self-reliant again instead of living a life where I felt I had to allow other people to provide for me. I wanted to create success so that I could be in a good space and *choose* the life that I wanted to live. I had dreams of success as an author, with a TV show, and as a teacher with a Spirit Talker Tribe following. The bravery of Bear Medicine helped me embody the person I wanted to become today, writing this book.

The bear represents courage and resilience, especially in the face of adversity. It's clear to me now, looking back on my life, Bear Medicine carried me through all of my struggles, even though I was not consciously aware that I carried it as my Power Totem. I didn't really know about Bear Medicine until I came back home to Nova Scotia, so all of these experiences were necessary for discovering who I am and my Totem Animals, so that I could step out in life.

Bear Medicine helps us overcome challenges through self-reliance and inner strength. It helps us trust our intuition and find the fortitude to overcome challenges within ourselves. I've learned to incorporate all those aspects of Bear Medicine through the healing work that I've done in my life and the strength and self-reliance that I've had to embody.

People who have Bear Medicine need to be on their own a lot. My life demands a lot of traveling, just like the bear in the wild. Bears are solitary creatures, and I feel that I've had to be a lone bear of sorts. I've had to create a life of abundance through all of it. I've had to embody a lot of courage and be very resourceful. Through this journey, I've gained a lot of wisdom, which has definitely heightened my intuition. I've had to do a lot of physical and emotional healing as well due to losses, including my first love when I was very young, my dad, my grandmother, my stepfather, Larry, and several relationships and marriages.

Bear Medicine is also about living a balanced life. When we learn to live with Bear Medicine, we have to be playful and assertive, learning to find the joy in life, but also to do what's needed. Bears embody this balanced approach to life. While they can be playful, most of the time they are very focused on providing for themselves. After all, they have a lot to do just to find enough food to sustain themselves. I do work a lot as well, but I set aside time to be playful and care for myself. As my life has moved along, I feel that I embody Bear Medicine a bit differently now. I have had the courage to face many adversities, develop the self-reliance and inner strength to sustain myself, and now I have found a more balanced life by working through this Bear Medicine. Using technology allows me to travel a bit less and enjoy the natural world surrounding me when I am not working. I feel more connected spiritually.

I think that spiritual people have to learn through all these changes and tough situations we all face in life. I have risen above it all, calling on the bravery, the strength, and the courage of the Bear to endure it. I feel that if Bear Medicine hadn't been a part of my life, I might have cowered and backed down and failed when faced with challenges in my past. I would have avoided things instead of dealing with them. I wouldn't have kept going, trying to succeed, or kept writing and teaching. Those challenges could have spiraled me down to a very dark place, but I said, "No, this is who I am, this is what I choose to do, and I am going to face my challenges with bravery, be as ferocious as I can be, and overcome this." I'm happy to say that I have. I have found my strength through it all by dealing with situations head-on. It has allowed me to broaden my career, become a Hay House author, continue as a speaker and teacher, and complete five seasons of my television show, *Spirit Talker*.

There is a lesson here for everyone who feels crippled by a situation that they did not see coming and that they have resisted dealing with: A challenge is the perfect time to invoke Bear Medicine and utilize that bravery that Bear offers and face these things head-on. It's important to remember that we can work with all Totem Animal Medicines, even if they are not our specific Totem Animals. When faced with adversity, we can call upon the Bear Medicine to find strength, courage, and resilience to embody this medicine within ourselves.

Prayer to the Spirit of the Bear

*Mighty Spirit of the Bear,
Guardian of the forest's heart,
I call upon your strength and wisdom,
To walk with me in courage and bravery.*

*You, who stand unshaken by the storms,
Teach me to stand firm in the face of fear.
You, who find power in solitude and silence,
Guide me to the wellspring of inner strength.*

*Bear of the mountains and valleys,
Lend me your fearless heart,
That I may face life's trials with boldness
And protect what I hold dear with unwavering resolve.*

*Grant me the courage to tread unknown paths,
To trust my instincts as you trust yours,
And to embrace both the light and shadow
That shape my journey and my soul.*

*Spirit of the Bear,
Walk beside me, within me, around me,
That I may grow strong in bravery,
And find balance in all that I do.*

*In your wisdom and power, I place my trust.
With gratitude and reverence, I honor you.*

Msit No'kmaq—All my relations.

♦ ♦ ♦ ♦

CHAPTER 18

♦ ♦ ♦ ♦ ♦

Kesaltultimkewey—Kitpu

LOVE—THE EAGLE

Eagle Medicine is the fourth teaching within the Seven Grandfather Teachings. Eagle Medicine is very powerful medicine. It's very spiritual medicine. Eagle could potentially be a Power Totem because of the eagle's ferociousness when it comes to hunting and protecting its nest. I've been to places where they have their nests, and I've seen hundreds of eagles there. I have a very special spot that I go to if I want to harvest feathers to gift to different people, if I choose to give them a feather.

  The reason we feel that they are so connected to love is that they fly higher and closer to Grandfather Sun, which is what we teach as the first sacred light, the first physical emanation of the light of our Creator that we see, the center of our solar system, just like every solar system in the universe encircles a star. Of all the birds in the world, eagles are one of those animals that fly closest to Grandfather Sun. Not many birds do this. There is an unconditional love where that light shines on them because they can fly higher than the clouds themselves. Eagle is able to connect most easily to the Creator and his unconditional love for us all. Eagle Medicine teaches us about the love of the Creator as seen through its eyes. In this way, Eagle is seen as a Spirit Totem that embodies Love. It is impossible to love others unless we truly love ourselves first. All love begins with love of self, and we can call upon Eagle Medicine when we seek the love that our Creator has for us all. It is through the sacredness of Love that all things are possible, and by fully loving ourselves we can more closely connect to the divine.

When there's a lightning storm, an eagle can literally fly above the clouds until the storm passes. So in this way, any situation beneath it that is difficult can be overcome; it rises above it and can see it and endure it in the safety of the clear skies above, until the storm passes and the eagle can land again, gently and safely. As humans, we may not see or fully understand the plan or the path we must follow that the Creator has for us in this life, but it is through the undeniable force of Love in the universe that we can grasp the unknowable. When we call upon Eagle Medicine, we can deepen our understanding of unconditional love, whether it is romantic, familial, or platonic. Eagle helps us deepen our love of self so that we can fully express love for others. Eagle represents Love because of the sacredness of love that the Creator shines upon it at all times, through all the storms and challenges of everyday life. This is why Indigenous people harvest the feathers of the eagle. This is why when an eagle feather comes to us, it is so sacred because it has been blessed by the Creator's light and unconditional love. That love is always there for the Eagle to embrace fully as it flies through the sky. The Eagle receives that light before any of us.

The Eagle embodies this unconditional love for itself but also for its family, and I've seen this in the eagle families that I've met throughout my life. Up near Truro, Nova Scotia, I've gone up to watch eagles nest. Their families are deeply connected. Even when the eagles have left the nest and flown off, they remain close to their eagle parents. Other birds in the Bird Nation in Canada leave their nests and fly off to join the flocks of birds that fly South for the winter. Eagles don't fly South. They stay in their territory. They stay on their land. The sacredness of the space from which they are born will endure all climates and all things that they must endure to stay in that space.

When I go there, I can see which ones are young because they still have brown and white feathers, they haven't turned black and white yet. They are adolescents, and they are going through the stages of the Medicine Wheel just like all of us. Even though the young have left their nests, and their parents have new babies in the nest from the current season, they still stay within a certain proximity to home until they become adults and then they can move out into the world themselves. Many of those young eagles are still flying not far from the nest. They don't interfere with their mother and the new young, but they are there because that is still their land, still their territory. They are very Indigenous to the sacred space from which they are born and in which they reside.

Their insight or foresight into life is just amazing. They see things that no one else can. If we can use their vision to face things in life, we will be able to have insight and foresight that is so far ahead of anyone else. That's why I feel that the natural spiritual medicine that the Eagle shares is so very important, especially when we need insight or foresight or specifically psychic abilities, because they have that vision that transcends beyond all other means of understanding. I feel like that's why Eagle is one of my predominant Totem Animals, because I have that insight, and that's why that medicine is with me in life. The unconditional love that they carry, which is so profound when learning it for ourselves, is given to us as we go through different life situations. We learn that unconditional love from all the different people that we meet and who come and go from our life. Many people have come and gone from my life, and I have loved them unconditionally and immensely, like Larry, my stepfather, being one of those people who has left my life.

One of the most profound expressions of love in relation to the Eagle came from my stepfather, Larry, after he had passed away. My mother had married him three years after my own father passed away, and for 18 years, Larry was a very important person to me. Even before Larry passed away, I had some insight into why he was not well. I saw a wisp of black smoke on the back of his head, and he was complaining of having a migraine. It kind of startled me when I saw the smoke; I wasn't sure what it meant right away, but not long afterward I learned that doctors had discovered that Larry had a massive tumor on the back of his brain.

I spent time with Larry, and I loved him through every step of that journey of going home to the spirit world. Even though Larry was my stepfather, I had that unconditional love for him. I loved him as a father. Although I lived in Alberta by the time he had married my mother, he would come out and visit me, and he even helped me build a deck and also helped me finish my basement, since he was very handy. He was also very analytical. He had been in the Air Force, and was just very good with tools and thinking and logic and things like that. I appreciated the medicine he brought to me in life and the logic with which he approached life, his intellect, his ability to think things through. We bonded very closely.

Larry knew what I did in life, but it wasn't something that he was completely open to, although as he got closer to the end, he called me the "blue man" because he could see the color of my aura. When doctors did the body scan, they discovered that cancer was all throughout his body and that his brain was actually the last place that the cancer had spread to. They performed emergency surgery to take the brain tumor out, but the cancer had metastasized through his whole spine and to every organ. It was evident that there was unfortunately no return from this disease.

What I could do, however, by using that Eagle Medicine, was to love him every step of the way until he went home. On his deathbed, just before he made his journey home to the spirit world, I had asked him to send me a message, a sign, not telling him specifically what I wanted. I just said, "Larry, you're going home soon now. Just come and let me know that you're okay if I don't get to see you tomorrow."

He was in the hospital in Truro, Nova Scotia, the place where I harvest eagle feathers to gift to other people. Those feathers are given to me by the family of eagles that I see up there. Larry went to Truro on September 9, 2010. I assumed that I would get to see him the next day, but I knew that his time was short. My mother and Larry had made an agreement that he would tell her when he needed to go to the hospital, and they agreed he would go to the one in Truro. My mom didn't feel comfortable with him passing away at home. She wanted doctors there to help him if he needed it. Larry woke up and said, "Truro" in a small voice, and I could tell that he was between this world and the next.

Very early the next morning, my mother called me to say that Larry had passed away. We were all very sad—my children, their mother, and I, and even my aunt Patsy, my mom's sister. We all got up and went with my mom to sit with his body for some time so we could all get to see him and say our good-byes before he was cremated.

As we were all driving in the car to the hospital in Truro, we were on the highway around the area of Sipekne'katik, an Indigenous community, not far from where the residential school was. As I was driving along the highway, I saw an eagle flying very high up in the sky as eagles do. I felt that it was connected to Larry, but when I told my aunt, "Patsy, look. Do you see the eagle in the sky? That brings us the message that Larry made it," she replied, "It's just an eagle, Shawn." I told her that it was more than that, but she didn't get it.

We kept driving along the highway, at 110 kilometers per hour, and I saw that the eagle flew lower and lower, closer and closer to our car. At one point, the eagle flew right in front of my car and turned sideways, full spread wing, facing my car! The tip of one wing touched the pavement in front of us and the other pointed straight up in the sky, and it looked at us for a brief moment. I had to jam on my brakes so I wouldn't hit it. Thankfully, there was no one behind me, and it flew back up in the sky as suddenly as it had flown down.

When I looked at Aunt Patsy, she was crying. I asked her, "Patsy, do you think it's just an eagle now, or do you think it might be a message?" I knew it was an unconditional loving message from Larry that said he was okay. She said it was the most profound spiritual experience she had ever had in her whole life. She said, "I've never had anything like that happen to me ever before." She was bawling in the car, not believing what had literally just happened.

When we arrived at the hospital, both of my children were holding Larry's hands, one of them even lay on the bed with him for a moment. I just put my hand on him. He was already starting to feel cold and rigor mortis was setting in. He was gone. He was no longer in his physical form. I know that there was a profound connection of love that day between us, our family, and Larry, with him letting us know that he was okay.

He even knew the strength and connection to my culture, sending me the eagle as the perfect messenger for me in that moment. When he was alive, he couldn't have known how deeply connected to Eagle Medicine I would become. Not long after that message from Larry, I would go on to find my first eagle feather, as well as all the other Eagle Medicines, and I would be given the Indigenous name that I carry today. I felt deeply happy and joyful knowing that even though I had lost him, he had found a unique and special way of connecting to me and my culture and my Totem Animal to let me know, "Hey, I'm okay, Shawn, I made it to where I need to be." I didn't even know how connected I was to the Eagle Nation at that point, because I hadn't even met the Elder who would teach me about it until after that. Larry knew, though. I didn't get my name White Eagle Spirit Talker until after that. Now I know that the Eagle Medicine is connected to me, but that story in itself was one of unconditional love and a message from someone I love and also one that is deeply connected to my Totem Animal and Medicine.

Prayer to the Spirit of the Eagle

Great Spirit of the Eagle,
Messenger of the heavens,
I call upon your soaring wisdom and grace,
To awaken in me the boundless love of the skies.

You, who see far beyond the horizon,
Teach me to see with a heart unclouded by judgment.
You, who ride the winds with unwavering trust,
Guide me to embrace the currents of love with courage.

Eagle of the boundless skies,
Lend me your vision to see the beauty within,
That I may love myself wholly,
And extend that love freely to others.

Help me to rise above fears and doubts,
To open my heart to the sacred unity of all beings.
Grant me the strength to forgive,
And the wisdom to cherish the light in everyone I meet so the light is all I see in every person I encounter.

Spirit of the Eagle,
Show me how to soar in the winds of compassion,
To love without conditions or limitations,
And to carry this divine love into every corner of my life.

With wings of gratitude, I honor your presence,
And with a heart full of love, I walk in life embodying your spiritual medicine.

Msit No'kmaq—All my relations.

CHAPTER 19

◆ ◆ ◆ ◆

Kepmite'lkaqn—Mestapekiejit

RESPECT—THE BISON OR BUFFALO

The fifth Grandfather Teaching is respect, and this is embodied by the bison, or buffalo as Indigenous people refer to this magnificent creature.

Buffalo teach the strength and endurance of things that they face in life, so we have to respect them, because a buffalo is not a creature that can be pushed around! They cannot be budged from a situation. Even bears and all other animals that approach buffalo have to have respect for the animal because of how strong they are. They carry great strength in their medicine.

In my oracle card deck, I explain the Sacred Grandfather Teaching of Respect, which suggests that we should take a balanced approach by being mindful of our thoughts and actions, which extends to our treatment of the Earth and all that inhabit it. By living honorably, we must not hurt others; rather, we should treat others the way we wish to be treated. Respect should be given freely from a heart-centered approach if we wish to be respected. What we put out into the world comes back to us.

I've actually seen buffalo in fields, how they herd together all their young to protect them, moving their calves into the middle and then surrounding them in a circle of protection. This way of sticking together and supporting each other through that unity is what gives the whole herd strength. As a community itself, buffalo have a strong sense of family. They will fight to the death if need be. They are ferocious animals.

Even my own memory of being in Sioux Valley, Manitoba, standing in the back of the pickup truck during the filming of *Spirit Talker*, was one that I will never forget. They were all around the truck and going past me. They are intimidating animals, just massive. They have this aura or personality of not seeming to be strong, but they are much stronger than we could possibly know. No matter where we are, if we need strength, unity, and support to help us go through challenges in life, Buffalo Medicine is absolutely good for that.

In Lakota, Buffalo is a symbol of abundance and manifestation so that we do not have to struggle to survive anymore. The symbolism of the birth of a sacred white buffalo is one of hope. It means good times are coming. The sacred medicine of a White Buffalo is one of optimism.

Vivienne is a Spirit Talker Tribe member, and she has a very strong connection to the White Buffalo as her Power Totem. It all began when she was just a girl growing up in South Africa. An Indigenous man from North America knocked on her door and spoke at length with her father about the Seven Grandfather Teachings, and he sold Vivienne's father a book all about these teachings. The Indigenous man shared stories about the White Buffalo Calf Woman, and ever since then, Vivienne has been drawn to these teachings and also to the wisdom of the Medicine Wheel. She is a psychotherapist who helps many people in her practice, and a shaman she once consulted has confirmed that the White Buffalo Totem is her Power Totem Animal and gives her strength in her life. She has visions of this White Buffalo spirit in the snow, and she can feel its head resting against hers, feel its breath, hear its hooves stamping in the snow. Hers is a very powerful and sacred connection that gives her strength and courage when serving her divine purpose.

Tracy, a Spirit Talker Tribe student, shared her very vivid dream of a white buffalo. She dreamed that she was being tracked and chased by a lot of people who had big sticks and clubs. She was running through the woods on a seemingly overgrown path, trying to outrun them. They seemed to get closer to her when she slipped and tumbled and slid on the grass and mud surrounding a lake. She felt helpless, defeated, unable to get up out of the deep mud. She thought the people chasing her would catch her for sure at that point. Lying there by the lake, helpless in the mud, she felt everything go dark and was unable to breathe. Just as she was ready to give up, she felt a huge energetic presence above her. When she opened her eyes, she saw a huge white buffalo above her. She felt the people chasing her fade away. The white buffalo gave her such an incredible feeling of being safe and being watched over. She closed her eyes in her dream and then she woke up.

I don't know what Tracy was going through in life when she had that dream, but I am reminded of my own dream of the dark shadowy figures running after me, wishing to do me harm, and then the seven white polar bears appearing from the woods and defeating them. That was a powerful dream of the White Polar Bear showing itself as my Power Totem Animal. In the same way, I feel that the White Buffalo might be Tracy's Power Totem Animal in life. The white color of the Buffalo represents purity in spirit. It is also a symbol of abundance, fertility, and the balance between nature and humanity.

Buffalo are great animals that provided for Indigenous people back in the day and were nearly hunted to extinction after first contact, when new settlers would hunt them for pelts and let everything else that Indigenous people would have harvested for food and such lay to waste instead. Now that balance that buffalo brought us in life, giving us life, because buffalo are life-givers, is returned in kind by Indigenous people.

When I went out West to film Season 4, Episode 6 of *Spirit Talker* in Tsuut'ina First Nation in Calgary, Alberta, I spent time with a herd of about 400 buffalo that they took care of. I had lived in Calgary for 17 years and had visited this community quite often. On this occasion, I was invited to take part in the annual buffalo roundup. There is a huge buffalo paddock there on their land, which is like a sanctuary within a large fenced-off area. Clayton Whitney was the paddock manager, and he cared for the buffalo all year round. His job was to "maintain the fences, the herd health, their grazing patterns, trying to keep them as natural as possible, just like they were in the old days," he said.

Every year, Clayton and the volunteer cowboys, a bunch of people from the Nation, would come out and help with the roundup. They ran approximately 400 buffalo through a system of corrals, vaccinated them, tagged them, and separated calves that they were going to be selling, some of which they harvested during the coming year.

A young Indigenous woman named Jordan Big Plume and I were on gate duty, and I was a little nervous about it. I just had to open and close the gate as the buffalo moved through the system of corridors. Once they had been vaccinated, it was important that they not go back in with the others that weren't vaccinated yet. From there they would get to go out in the field and join the herd again.

They had to blindfold the buffalo because when they were blindfolded, once they had been corralled into a metal enclosure called the squeeze, they would calm down enough to get their vaccine—of course using a very long needle—get dewormed, and then released back to the herd and to freedom for another year. It is a very dangerous job. They are much different from cattle because they are so wild and very stressed. They can start banging and crashing into things. It's pretty incredible to see how powerful they are.

Jordan Big Plume explained that the community feels very blessed to have the herd there and that it is a way to keep them really close to their spirituality and their community. Clayton says they are so lucky to have such a big herd on their Nation. He hopes that the herd will grow and that someone else will come along who feels as strongly as he does about looking after them. Tsuut'ina is a massive Nation in terms of land mass, and the buffalo can't be looked after alone, but they manage to work through it as a team. All the volunteers and rugged cowboys who pitch in to help do it from their heart, for the community, for the buffalo, and for themselves. I am very proud to have taken part in this because it is not a small job, and I feel I did my part in taking care of the buffalo.

Buffalo have given us care for so many decades, so now it's our turn to give back to the buffalo, so that they can continue to live their life. I do know that Indigenous people may still harvest a buffalo from time to time, but they will only harvest what the community can have as a food offering. Buffalo teach us respect, because we are still caring for this sacred animal in Indigenous communities. We show our respect for the life that they have given us by giving back their life. That is why we care for them.

Prayer to the Spirit of the Bison and Buffalo

Great Spirit of the Bison and Buffalo,
Ancient ones of strength and resilience,
I approach you with humility and respect,
Seeking the wisdom you carry in your great being.

You, who walk the Earth with steady steps,
Teach me the balance of patience and perseverance,
To move forward with purpose and grace,
As you have done across the sacred plains.

Guardians of abundance and community,
You provide life and sustenance to many.
Help me honor the interconnected web of all beings
And tread lightly upon this Earth, as you do.

Mighty ones, whose spirits endure through trials,
Grant me the courage to weather the storms of life.
Guide me to stand strong in my truth
And carry the weight of my responsibilities with dignity.

With every breath I honor you,
With every step I give thanks for your teachings.
May your wisdom and spiritual medicine of respect flow
through my heart
And your strength dwell within my body and soul.

May I always walk in harmony with your spirit,
With respect for all life, and gratitude for every blessing.
Aho, Wela'lioq Tatanka—Thank you, Bison and Buffalo Nation,
For your gifts of Respect, Strength, and Connection.

Msit No'kmaq—All my relations.

CHAPTER 20

♦ ♦ ♦ ♦

Ns+tuo'qn—Kopit

WISDOM—THE BEAVER

Wisdom is the sixth Grandfather Teaching, and it is embodied by the Beaver. I can clearly understand why, as I've observed many beavers in the wild. Yes, beavers have large, sharp teeth, and they're impeccable swimmers. But their wisdom is innate. When they sense danger nearby, they'll alert others by splashing the water loudly with their tail. Their impressive dams are also much more complex than we might think, and serve to create a safe pond for their community.

I also learned about the beaver through being in Beavers, Cubs, and Scouts as I was growing up. These are part of an association for young boys who are growing up and learning about nature, character development, leadership, and fitness. In Britain and Canada, the names for the different levels were taken from Rudyard Kipling's *The Jungle Book*. Cubs could represent a baby bear, wolf, or lion. I remember thinking it was kind of cool that we had Beavers, Cubs, and then Scouts as a progression through the years. Beavers was my first connection to that group. I got together with some friends at school and joined. We even dressed like beavers because we had hats that had tails on the back of them. We were taught about a great silver beaver, and we learned myths and stories about it.

In Beavers we were taught that if there were predators around, the beaver would slap its huge flat tail on the water and make a really loud noise, not only to protect themselves but to warn all the other Beaver Nation and all the other forest animals that danger was near. It is a message that says, "Tread lightly; be careful!" They were not only mindful of their own immediate environment but also of all the surrounding environment as well.

The reason they carry the teaching of wisdom is that when they move into a certain waterway, they change it. They change the area through architecture. The architecture of the grand design that is written within their DNA is their wisdom. Nothing can describe it, and it is passed down and it is embedded within them to cut down trees in a very particular way. If we ever have the chance to watch a beaver at work, we can appreciate how very intelligent they are, much more than we can imagine.

Their wisdom is evident even when they are chopping down trees. They are smart enough to know that when carving grooves into the trunk with their teeth, they will chew to a certain place in the tree, and then after so many chews, they will actually stop and listen every few moments to see if the tree is making a cracking sound. They are very mindful of the danger that is present in the act of gnawing down a tree, and they have to listen to make sure they are not in danger as the whole tree comes crashing down. As soon as the tree cracks and begins to fall, the beaver runs quickly to safety.

Beavers build these great architectural waterways following a grand design that they carry in their DNA. They create canals through the water that help them float the branches needed to build their lodge. They build dams using the trees that they break down. The architecture of a beaver dam is quite impressive. Some people, particularly farmers, might say that the beaver is ruining the environment, but they are actually creating a natural environment rich in diversity. They are creating a new environment in which a lot of fish and other wildlife can go to get water, and they change waterways in such a way that they would corral fish in that area. Beavers, being strict vegetarians, don't eat fish themselves. They eat bark, leaves, twigs, buds, and aquatic vegetation. The whole beaver family will gather their favorite woody foods and bury their cache in their lodge to see them through the winter months. Beavers enter their lodge through openings that are only accessed underwater. In this way, they can keep safe from predators.

When I was a young boy, I used to go fishing about three and a half miles behind my mom's house. I came across a beaver dam, and that's where I would sometimes fish from, standing on top of the beaver dam. The water was so deep, and that's where the big trout were. I was always mindful that beavers would create these ecosystems that would make fishing easier for me! I also saw many types of wildlife that would come there to drink, like deer, raccoons, foxes, and coyotes. I've seen ducks and geese gather in those places too. To humans, however, beaver dams are not good sources of drinking water because beaver droppings are not good for us and can make us sick with beaver fever.

Beaver dams themselves also filter water. The water that seeps through a dam and continues on the other side on its journey is filtered through and becomes somewhat cleaner on its way out. The streams and rivers are cleaner because pollutants like nitrogen and phosphorus are filtered naturally. Their dams also help prevent flooding and erosion. All of these good things are brought about in the environment by beavers building dams.

The beaver represents wisdom in the Seven Grandfather Teachings because it uses its innate gifts for survival and alters its environment in a sustainable and beneficial way for the entire ecosystem. Beaver Medicine helps us make carefully considered decisions on what best suits everyone rather than just focusing on ourselves, helping us be mindful that the choices we make will impact the next seven generations. We can call upon Beaver Medicine when making decisions that contribute not only to our own development but also to the development of a peaceful and healthy environment, community, and ecosystem. Prudence, intelligence, and practicing good judgment all belong to the wisdom of the beaver.

Just as the beaver makes decisions that bring benefits to all in the ecosystem, so too are our decisions affecting everyone else around us in a spiritual sense, because we are all one. Beaver Medicine is present in everyone who thinks about our natural environment and our ecosystem that surrounds us all and cares for the world itself. What we do today will have ripple effects for the next seven generations after us. If we all carried that wisdom and understanding about the cause and effect of what we do, using our knowledge as well as our wisdom to realize the effect that we have on our environment, the world would be a better place. Beavers understand this and create a sustainable ecosystem that benefits all that they are surrounded by. With their actions, they clear the forest so that new growth can come in, as it always does. They don't take too much from the forest, only enough to create the ecosystem that will benefit the generations of wildlife coming after them.

Beavers mate for life and are monogamous and have offspring that go off and create new ecosystems in the environment after a couple of years of living within their family. They are very territorial, so they will be sure to venture far from their family of origin and continue the work of benefiting the larger area.

I think it's amazing to watch them very intentionally and intelligently taking down trees and very deliberately placing specific pieces of wood to strengthen their dam and their lodge. There is a lot of thinking that goes into it, but of course it is all innate wisdom, wired into their DNA from thousands of years of evolution that has brought them to this way of survival. Their behavior helps the world and does not destroy the world.

Beavers teach us to use our gifts wisely and to live by them. They also represent patience and determination. If we carry Beaver Medicine, we may find ourselves to be the type of person who needs to learn more about persistence and being more determined in life. Persistent and determined people likely carry Beaver Medicine. People who are architects draw from Beaver wisdom, as well as builders and designers and engineers, those who are very logical in their thinking who use their intelligence for the creation of something in life. I feel like a lot of engineers, interior designers and decorators, and people who love working in construction, who are very constructive and creative, are probably very naturally connected to the Beaver and may not even know it.

"Busy as a beaver" is a saying because beavers are not ones to be idle. They are very busy, persistent, and determined workers who keep going until the job is finished. They never quit halfway through. Those who carry Beaver Medicine are creative and stubborn. They understand the importance of cooperation, unity, and using their individual talents to create their environment.

Prayer to the Spirit of the Beaver

Great Spirit of the Beaver,
Master builder and keeper of the waters,
I approach you with reverence and an open heart,
Seeking your wisdom and the strength of your teachings.

You who shape the land with purpose and care,
Teach me the art of creating with intention,
To build my life with thoughtfulness and harmony,
And to honor the balance of work and rest.

Keeper of ingenuity and resourcefulness,
Show me how to use my gifts wisely,
To craft solutions where obstacles arise,
And to recognize the tools I already hold within.

Wise one who understands the flow of the river,
Guide me to discern when to act and when to wait,
To know the difference between what serves and what hinders,
And to align my efforts with the natural rhythm of life.

Guardian of connection and community,
Remind me of the strength in unity,
And the importance of tending to my relationships,
As you tend to your family and home.

With every ripple in the water, I honor your spirit.
With every step, I give thanks for your guidance.
May your wisdom flow through my Heart Sacred Fire and Spirit,
And your wisdom and knowledge guide my path.

Wela'lioq, Kopit—Thank you, Beaver Nation,
For your teachings of Wisdom
May I walk in harmony with your spirit,
And always honor the sacred waters of life.

Msit No'kmaq—All my relations.

◆ ◆ ◆ ◆

CHAPTER 21

♦ ♦ ♦ ♦

Teliaqewey—Maqsitate'w
HONESTY—SABE OR BIGFOOT

In different parts of the country this interdimensional creature is known as Sabe, Bigfoot, or Sasquatch. In the Indigenous language of the West Coast, where Sabe is commonly known, he is known as Sasquits. The name Sasquatch comes from the Indigenous name Sasquits. Since being there on the West Coast, I feel like I have a much stronger and greater connection to Sasquits.

Sasquits represents honesty. That is because in the Sacred Grandfather Teachings, it starts with oneself, our person, and it takes bravery to be honest through our words and actions. By being honest with ourselves it becomes easier to be honest with others. We have to be honest with ourselves. If not, we fool ourselves. The Sacred Grandfather Teaching of Honesty is provided to us by Sasquits, who imparts his ability to truly understand what he is and how he walks through life. To walk with integrity is to know honesty, and to be honest with oneself reflects a level of righteousness.

Long ago, Sasquits walked among people to remind them to be honest with each other and to the laws of the Creator. It is said that honest people keep their promises, and living a life true to oneself exemplifies honesty. To truly accept who we are and how the Creator made us is to be true to one's own spirit. Fully accepting who we are will guide us through this sacred teaching.

Indigenous people in particular are deeply connected to Sasquits. He is one of our sacred Spirit Animals. Even though I don't feel him physically walking through life, I do feel that he is an interdimensional being. I think it's amazing that in Indigenous culture we have a being that once walked upon the Earth but no longer walks upon the Earth like we do in physical form. That doesn't mean that as an interdimensional being he can't take on physical form for short periods of time, very much like my own spirit guides have at different times. They exist in spirit, and yet I've met my guides physically, and they have walked beside me for a moment. I've seen them walk around me, and I've spoken to them, and I couldn't even tell that they weren't real, physical people until they vanished without leaving a trace. I think there's a similarity with Sasquits. He walks between two worlds. He does appear at different times to certain people, and he has been seen.

I had an amazing experience when I was filming *Spirit Talker*, Season 4, Episode 13, in the community of Sts'ailes, about 100 miles from Vancouver, British Columbia. These people really embrace Sasquits. The symbol for their community is Sasquits, and they celebrate him, and they even protect a sacred trail that they call the Sasquits Trail.

I met with one of their Elders named Willie Charles. He told me that *Sts'ailes* means "beating heart." The word *Sasquits* derives from the language of the Sts'ailes First Nation people. He also explained that Sasquits is a shape-shifter and can become anything: a tree, a rock, a bird, an animal. He is a supernatural being, or slalekum. Elder Charles went on to say that some people believe that he can vanish. Their belief is that he can go from the physical world to the spiritual world.

He can walk between the two realms. That is why he is called a slalekum, and his name is Sasquits.

The young people even have a ceremony and a special dance. I was there to observe them. Some of the children were as little as two years old, and they all had their ceremonial dress and sacred objects while doing one of their special dances. The Sasquits dance, done by the older children, was definitely my favorite. They were wearing their own unique masks that they had made to look like their versions of how Sasquits may have appeared to them in different ways. It was kind of creepy seeing these kids walking around, arms and legs stiff, lumbering around to the beat of the drum, because the journey song of the drum and the chanting that they did was a bit scary. It was still very entertaining and fun, though, as they exemplified Sasquits himself. They looked like they were sneaking around in a circle as they were moving just like Sasquits. They would come and go.

My experience was really amazing in Sts'ailes First Nation, seeing people celebrating Sasquits like that. I felt that they had a deep connection. There are even some petroglyphs of Sasquits somewhere up on a hill that predate contact. I feel that there is a belief in Sasquits that existed long before people came into contact with what we call the New World. First Nations people have always known about the spirit of Sasquits. They honored his journey, and I feel like even today, Sasquits is cherished and honored in funny ways as well. I saw a T-shirt that said he is the "World's Hide and Seek Champion." They still can't find him to this day!

It is almost counterintuitive that Sasquits should be taught as representing honesty when those who have seen him have been called liars by so many who do not believe in his existence. I myself have had my own experience of Sasquits. I didn't see him in physical form like many people have seen him. However, what I did see was an apparition of Sasquits. I believe that he appeared to me. It was really kind of surreal, but after that experience, I felt that I shared the mystery of Sasquits with so many others who have also claimed to have seen him.

There are massive cedar trees in British Columbia where the Sts'ailes First Nation is. What I saw there were these big cedars along the Sasquits Trail. I went out into the forest among the giant cedar trees, and I laid out some tobacco. I asked the Great Spirit to show me Sasquits. I went for a walk down the Sasquits Trail for a while, not really expecting to see him, but hoping that I would.

Then, to my amazement, I saw what looked almost like a spirit in the shape of Sasquits run out of one cedar tree, run across the path, and run into another cedar tree and disappear! It was a blurry silhouette of a hairy and magnificent creature that I can only surmise was the spirit of Sasquits. I actually had to stop and take a moment and say, "Did I really just see what I just saw?" because again, the "World's Hide and Seek Champion" appeared for a moment and then disappeared the next moment, and I couldn't find him, and I couldn't find any tracks either. He was just gone!

I think Sasquits appears to help us to remember we have to be honest with ourselves. We have to accept ourselves. If we are really being honest, we accept ourselves for who we are in life and what we are here to do, who we are here to *be*. As odd-looking as Sasquits is, he, too, has to accept himself as the spiritual, interdimensional being that he embodies within our world to show us that it's okay to be who we really are, no matter whether people believe us or not, or whether they think we're ugly or not. We have to be honest with ourselves and love ourselves unconditionally. We must know that we are one of the Creator's beings and that we have a divine purpose for being here, just as Sasquits also has a purpose. The medicine that he shares when he does appear would be for specific reasons, namely his honesty.

If we have Sasquits appearing in our life in different ways, maybe we need to be honest in a situation. We have to be honest with our appearance, and we have to love the appearance that we see reflected back at us in the mirror. We must accept ourselves because of that honesty. We must accept where we are in life, our situations that we are in, with the people that we face. We have to be really honest with how we approach life, because Sasquits is a sacred creature, deeply connected to Indigenous people, but he honestly knows that if he were to be seen in some way, that it is intentional. He is not showing himself to people by accident.

There are so many cultures around the world that also have very similar Spirit Animals to Sasquits. I think they may all embody the same medicine of Honesty. In Chinese culture, the dragon is part of their horoscope. It is part of their culture and maybe dragons have existed upon the Earth in the past. Perhaps when people have said that they have seen dragons at times, it was an ancient spirit of a dinosaur that could fly, maybe a relative of the pterodactyl, and that they've been called dragons.

It might be that Sasquits existed in the physical world in the past as an ancient humanoid being that was very tall, had lots of strength, fur, and was somewhat ape-looking. Maybe Sasquits was oddly ape-looking but not exactly like an ape itself. Maybe there was an evolution there that ended. Throughout the millions of years that the Earth has been in existence, there have been species that have come and gone, but that doesn't mean that their spirits aren't still deeply connected to Mother Earth. They may appear to different people at different times because there are different levels of energy within the spirit world itself.

The Yeti in Tibet, for example, which has appeared to those people, looking like a primitive, prehistoric-looking white creature, might have walked the Earth at some point in time and people have sometimes caught glimpses of it. The Loch Ness Monster, or Nessie, is another creature that people have claimed to have seen. It was an ancient dinosaur that existed. How do we know when people get a visit from Ogopogo in the Okanagan Lakes of British Columbia that it isn't a sighting of an ancient sea creature that existed during the age of dinosaurs? There is a similar creature, called Champy that people have seen in Lake Champlain in upstate New York and Vermont.

Regardless, I feel like for moments, there is no time and we get to see things that may transcend time. It could be a dragon; it could be a Sasquits; it could be a Yeti or a Loch Ness-type creature. I think different cultures have had different experiences like that because their spirits were also connected to Mother Earth, so it's not too strange to think that they may visit at times or still mingle within different dimensions and maybe appear in our dimension here and there.

Whatever mythical creature that has existed, I think people struggle to tell anyone that they saw something like that for fear of being perceived to be lying, even though they are being honest. I think the medicine they bring to us is being truthful and honest in what we say and how we approach life, no matter what. If anyone challenges us, we must remember that we can call upon the medicine of Sasquits to help us be who we need to be and help us be honest with ourselves, and not let anyone else's expectations or opinions blur that truth in any way. What we experience is our truth, and it may not be the same as that of others, but we have to be honest about our experiences and how we approach others. Sasquits is a reminder to us that we must own our truth, even if people don't believe us.

I am a psychic medium and spirit talker, and as such, I see a lot of things that other people don't see. I don't worry about what people think is true or not. I speak my truth because it's the way I've seen it. It's the way I've experienced it, and sometimes I have to call upon the medicine of Sasquits to help me be the person I am and say the things I need to say. I know my experiences, and I honestly have to teach and tell people about them, because that's going to help expand their awareness and understanding of life. That medicine can help us in our understanding.

Since being in Sts'ailes and having that apparition of Sasquits going from one cedar to another and seeing the Sasquits dancers, I now have a fascination with him that I have never had before. I saw him myself, so I know that he was a real being that was in this world, and I know that I have to honor the medicine that he brings within the Seven Grandfather Teachings, the medicine of Honesty.

WALKING WITH YOUR SPIRIT TOTEM ANIMALS

Prayer to Sabe (Bigfoot)

Great Spirit of Sabe, Keeper of Honesty,
I come before you with a humble heart,
Seeking your guidance and the wisdom of your ancient path.

You, who walk the forests unseen yet present,
Teach me to live with truth in every step I take.
Help me honor my words and actions,
That they may align with the integrity of my spirit.

Guardian of the unseen and the mysterious,
Reveal to me the power of honesty,
To see myself as I truly am,
And to stand firmly in my authentic truth.

Wise one of the wild places,
Guide me to discern the paths I should walk,
To shed the masks that no longer serve me,
And to speak with clarity and courage when others remain silent.

Teacher of connection and respect,
Help me honor the sacred bond between all beings,
To walk lightly upon this Earth and tread with respect,
Just as you move in harmony with the natural world.

I honor your spirit with every truth spoken.

I give thanks for your guidance.
I ask wholeheartedly that your Spiritual Medicine and wisdom
flow freely within my life, and that honesty guides my path.

Wela'lin—Thank you, Sabe,
For your teachings of honesty, humility, and authenticity.
May I walk in harmony with your spirit
And always honor the truth within myself and others.

Msit No'kmaq—All my relations.

CHAPTER 22

♦ ♦ ♦ ♦

Tia'muwe'ka'timkewey
THE MOOSE HARVEST

I began the first chapter with stories of hunting and how an encounter with a rabbit made me rethink my attitude and my actions toward the Animal Nation. I then decided I would not hunt anymore. I spoke about how my father and I would go hunting together, and no matter how many times we would go out to hunt for a deer or big game, there was nothing. Not even once. Then my father passed away unexpectedly, and my opportunity to harvest a big game animal with him was lost forever.

However, one night while working on this book, I had a dream. I was standing in a field and there was a herd of moose there. At the beginning of the dream, I thought to myself, "Is Spirit trying to tell me that the Moose is one of my Spirit Totem Animals that I don't know about?" There was nothing really profound about the dream except for me standing and looking at moose in a field. I know that Moose Medicine encourages us to protect and respect the natural world, showing us that our well-being is connected to the well-being of all living things in our environment. Moose Medicine encourages us to explore our inner strength as well. Still, I wasn't convinced that the moose was trying to reveal itself to me as one of my Animal Totems.

Shortly after, I got a call from a woman named Juliet, an Elder in Listuguj, Quebec, near the New Brunswick border. It is a Mi'kmaq reserve and is about a six-hour drive from where I live right now. Juliet's husband, Conrad, is a hunting guide, although he is not Indigenous. She called me out of the blue and spoke to my wife, Michelle. I had been talking to my wife about wanting to eat better in life, to have better quality food, because as we get older we want to take better care of ourselves. We have been looking for healthier food sources, so we grew vegetables in our own garden this year.

When Juliet told me about moose hunting, I told her about my dream. She said, "You should come moose hunting." I told her that I did not have a license, and she told me that as an Indigenous person in Canada, I don't need a license as long as an Elder who brings the gun has a license and gives it to me with explicit permission to use it. Michelle and I talked about it, and we felt that maybe this would be a much better food source than going to buy meat at a store.

With store-bought meat, we don't know how the animals have been treated before slaughter and how they've been managed up to that point. Also, we knew that if we were able to harvest a moose, that we would have an animal that would have no cholesterol and would be very healthy. With moose meat we could make our own hamburger, steaks, roasts, and stew meat. We would put it in our freezer, which we had to go out and buy specially for the moose meat that we would harvest. We knew the entire freezer would be completely full with this animal. They are such large animals; they can feed a family for a year.

As a young person growing up, even though I had never hunted a moose ever in my life, my uncle had, and I helped him to harvest the meat. I remember that meat being the best I had ever eaten and close in flavor to beef. So I decided to go to New Brunswick, even though I had a very short window of opportunity with it being close to Christmas.

Once out there, my hunting guide Conrad and I took a drive out to his and Juliet's cabin in New Brunswick. We looked around on Crown Land for any traces of moose. There were some tracks, which we saw when we went out on his side-by-side, which he called "The Beast" because it had six wheels and a big bucket on it. We even saw moose tracks inside our own tracks when we drove by, so there were definitely moose in the area.

The next morning we got up to look around again with my wife, Michelle, and the Elder Juliet also came along with me and our guide, Conrad. He taught me about how to handle the hunting rifle that we would be using, about ammunition, safety, shooting, and how to use the tripod for the rifle and the whole nine yards. It was the first day of our hunt and within the first hour, I knew we were on to something.

My guide didn't think that we were in the right spot to find any moose, but suddenly I had a vision of moose tracks. I said, "Did we come by here earlier and see any moose tracks?" He said no. I answered that it was so strange because I was psychically seeing moose tracks in my mind. No sooner did I say that when he said, "Look up on the hill! There are five or six moose up there!" It was like I had a psychic vision about where the moose would be when I went by there.

It was very much like the dream I had about the moose when we came upon that clearing. We saw five or six moose that were standing in the field. The guide told me that it was up to me, but if I were going to harvest a moose for food, now would be a good time to do it! We set up the rifle on the tripod and I stood up on an embankment. Through the scope, we could see the moose, which were very far away. He told me how to use the rifle and scope very accurately by showing me which notches I should be aiming for. Some of the moose were much larger than others. There were some bull moose in the field, as well as some female cows. I wasn't shooting an animal for a trophy, so I didn't necessarily want to shoot a bull and keep its antlers. My guide said I could go for one of the bulls. I said, "No, the one that presents itself to me will be the one that I will shoot for the harvest."

One large female stood out and turned completely sideways to me in the clearing. I felt that it was a sign for me that if I were to take a moose, then I should take that one. It was like she presented herself to me to harvest. It was like everything just aligned to happen the way it should to make that possible. There were no branches or trees blocking my shot. She was pretty far away, 535 yards away to be precise. My rifle, a .30-06, was steady on the tripod, so I aimed and took my first shot. I hit the moose, but she did not go down yet. A couple more shots felled her right where she stood. She hardly seemed aware of what was happening, so I knew she had not suffered. Strangely, the other moose just walked away.

We left her there for a while so she could have space and time to make her journey home to the spirit world. When we came back later, I brought my sacred tobacco offering with me. She was very far away, and we actually had a hard time finding her, because even though she fell in the exact spot where I had shot her, that was over 500 yards away from where we had stood and she blended in with the environment.

I knelt down beside the moose, and while my guide went back to get his side-by-side, I had about 10 minutes with her alone. She was deceased, had moved into the spirit world. I took out my tobacco pouch that I brought with me in the hopes that I would hunt a moose, and I held it in my hand over my heart, I held it up to the spirit world, I laid some on the ground where she was, and I offered it to the animal. I offered her my love and my gratitude, thanking her for the life that she had given to provide food for me. I expressed gratitude for the life that she had lived, as well as the opportunity to harvest the meat for my family. I laid the tobacco on her heart, on her head as well. I placed my hands on her heart, placed my hands on her head, and I was joyful but also a little sad for her, but mostly I just felt happy and grateful.

I told her that when I make my journey home, I would like to meet her in the spirit world, because I know all animals go to Spirit. I felt Spirit had sent me there that day to have the opportunity to harvest an animal in a humane way, as my ancestors had done in the past. I prayed for her spirit, and I thanked her for the sacrifice that she had made for me for the food that she was offering for me and my family. I knew that she didn't suffer, because when she fell to the ground she was immediately gone, not trying to move or budge at all. It made me feel better that she did not suffer.

My guide and the Elder came back, and they squeezed one of her nipples. There was no milk there, so she was past the age of having any calves. It made sense because she was so large, almost as large as a bull moose in the field that I saw. She was at the end stage of her life, and she was much larger than she had appeared through the scope from 500 yards away. My guide guessed her weight to be about 750 to 800 pounds. He taught me how to skin and quarter the moose before we could bring it back with us. We literally picked every bit of meat off the animal and wasted nothing. Any parts of her that we could not use ourselves, we offered to the Animal Nation to feed off.

My guide taught me all about harvesting the moose and all the work that went into harvesting the animal once we brought it back to Listuguj. He knew how to hang it before it could be butchered for meat. It hung in his garage for a week to give the quarters time to drain at the perfect temperature, before we went back and butchered it for packaging. It was then ready to be used for all sorts of dishes.

Since coming home, I've had some of the meat, and when I ate it, I gave the animal as much gratitude as I had when I hunted her. I felt enormous joy, in the sense that I felt that this meal was really healthy for me. I also knew that the life of the animal was a good one in the wild, not being constrained by any fences, and wasn't harmed in any horrible way, like in a slaughterhouse. With every bite that I take of this moose that I've harvested, I am grateful. I am grateful for every bite. It has made me appreciate the food that I eat even more. I feel good when I eat it.

Coming home from New Brunswick with my moose meat in the truck, I thought about my dad. Hunting was one of the things we would do together, and he taught me about hunting appropriately and honorably. One of the things we were never able to do was get a large animal ourselves, but I felt like my dad was with me that day. When I got in the car to drive home, one of the songs that my dad used to play on the guitar, which is even my ringtone on my phone right now, "House of the Rising Sun" by the Animals, was playing on the radio of my truck. It was the first song that came on. It came on satellite radio, and it is not a song that plays often. I hadn't heard it on the radio in a long, long time. I felt that it was a message from my dad.

I felt like my dad was with me on this hunt, and I felt like the spirit world had guided me to do the hunt and aligned everything so that it could happen. The fact that it took place before this book was finished is very significant, so I could include this story and show how the experience of hunting with my father has come full circle. Between the dream, the Elder calling me, the psychic vision, and the moose presenting herself to me, it was all meant to be. Also, my hunting guide has the wisdom of an Elder in terms of his knowledge about hunting and harvesting moose, just like my father had. He showed me how to humanely hunt and harvest an animal and how to respect an animal, just like my father and other Elders had taught me. I blessed the animal according to my culture, I thanked the animal and made a medicine offering for the animal, and every time I have a meal, I will be forever grateful for the sacrifice that she gave to me and my family.

Hippocrates wrote, "Let food be thy medicine, and medicine be thy food." So much of the food that we eat, we eat mindlessly, without thinking about the spirit of the animal that we are eating and without thinking about the nutritional effects or consequences of what we are eating. We need to be mindful of the food that we eat. We also often don't remember to stop and thank the animal or the plant we are eating for sacrificing its physical form for our sustenance.

In Indigenous culture, we see all things as having a spirit, whether we eat meat or don't eat meat and we are vegetarian or vegan. We should be grateful for the fruits, vegetables, and all the plants that we are eating. It is very important that we honor the spirit in all things. All things have a spirit, including the apples on the apple tree, the blueberries that we pick, the lettuce that we pull from our garden, in addition to all the animals that we eat. Some people reading this book might think that eating animals goes against the spiritual connection that they may have with them, but we have to remember that when we have a meal, we have to thank the animal for the life that it has given us and the sustenance that it provides for us. If it's not an animal, then we should thank the lettuce, thank the trees, thank the plants, thank our garden with every meal, thank the food. When we are mindful when we eat, there is an energy there that is present in how we eat.

For example, when we eat food that we know is not good for us and we think, *Oh, this is horrible for me!*, what does that do to our body? Even though people might disagree with hunting, I feel that they might go buy meat at the store and have no ethical awareness about it. I feel like I have taken ownership for my food, and I feel like I am doing it as ethically as I possibly can. If we don't have that opportunity to hunt for our food, then we can at least thank the spirit of the animal whose flesh we have chosen to eat, thanking it for providing sustenance for us in this life. Giving thanks for our food should not be something that we only do at Thanksgiving but with every meal we are privileged to have.

Prayer of Gratitude for Food

*Creator, Great Spirit, I give thanks for this meal before me.
For the life of the plants, for the life of the animals,
I offer my gratitude.
I honor their sacrifice, knowing that their spirit now becomes
a part of me.*

*To Mother Earth, who cradled these gifts in her soil,
To the Waters, who nourished them with life,
To Grandfather Sun, who gave warmth and strength,
And to the hands that gathered and prepared this meal,
I give my thanks.*

*May I receive this food with respect and humility.
May it bring strength to my body, clarity to my mind, and kindness
to my heart.
May I walk in life in a good way, using this energy to do what is right,
And honor the connection that we all share.*

*Wela'lioq, Msit No'kmaq.
I thank you. All my relations.*

◆ ◆ ◆ ◆

CHAPTER 23

♦ ♦ ♦ ♦

Etek na Ajiwjutasimk Ajiwjutasimkewey wjit Wais+sk

THERE IS ALWAYS HOPE AT HOPE FOR WILDLIFE

Hope for Wildlife is a nonprofit wildlife rehabilitation center in Nova Scotia that is just down the road from where I live. I mentioned this rescue center in a previous chapter when I wrote about a crow that came to my house one day and walked right up to me and stood on my shoe as I sat outside with my friend Grant. That crow was an escapee from the center, but he was not seen or found again after his little visit to me. The whole team at Hope for Wildlife had shown up to search for that missing crow, but their search was unsuccessful.

Hope Swinimer founded Hope for Wildlife in 1997 on a farm. It wasn't long before her efforts got the attention of TV producers, and the television series *Hope for Wildlife* was born in 2009. The show runs in over 20 countries around the world. The aim of this center is to rescue and rehabilitate wildlife so it can be released back into the wilderness. From the time of its opening until 2024, the center has saved around 90,000 animals of 250 different species and has successfully returned them into the wild.

Some of the animals, however, have never forgotten the care and attention that they have received and have been known to show up for unexpected visits. On occasion, some creatures end up becoming permanent residents, like Tilly the crow, who showed up at the center wearing nail polish on her talons. I don't think she especially liked having her talons painted by perhaps a woman, but I am only guessing. She hates all women but loves men, and she especially loves me and purrs and bows her head so I can pet her. We have a special bond.

I went to visit Hope at her center, and when I told her I was working on a book about Animal Totems, she immediately said that her Spirit Totem was the marten. She has a special spirit connection to the marten, and they will always have a place in her heart. She had cared for a female marten named Gretel who lived a full and healthy life, up to the age of 17. Hope never thought that another marten would come to her in her lifetime because it is so rare for martens to be found in the wild, but miraculously a gentleman who knew about Hope for Wildlife found one and knew about Hope for Wildlife and contacted her for help. She immediately bonded with the little marten that desperately needed care. He had survived an encounter with a porcupine, and so Hope named this little marten "Quill."

Quill the marten had run up to a gentleman, who as it happened knew that it was a marten and not a mink, which is an easy mistake to make. He was looking for help, and he was full of quills. The man phoned Hope at Hope for Wildlife and said the marten was sitting on his shoulder as they spoke and that he would bring him right over. Hope thought that he must be a mink because people often confuse the two. When Hope pulled the little marten out of the box, she saw that not only was he really a marten, but he was also full of quills from top to bottom. They were in his heart, in his lungs, everywhere, but he was still very much alive! He wasn't growling or wanting to attack, which would have been normal for a wild marten.

After successfully removing the quills, the Hope for Wildlife team realized that Quill had lots of other issues, including a heart murmur. Strangely, this marten was never scared, never nervous to be around humans. The gentleman who rescued him drove four hours to get there, and the marten sat on his shoulder for most of the drive. Hope thought it had to have been hand-raised, so she wrote a letter to the government asking permission to keep it at Hope for Wildlife for education for two reasons: the first being that he didn't have a sound body or heart and the second being that he was imprinted, because it was obvious that he had been raised by humans.

Quill was nursed back to health over the next five or six months, and Hope waited to hear back from the government. The rules had changed since she had had Gretel, and she wanted to make sure everything was done legally. The marten thrived and was so affectionate and playful, he was just like a little puppy. He followed her around and let her pet him and never left her side.

Unfortunately, Hope was not allowed to keep him, because pine martens are an endangered species in Nova Scotia, and so Quill had to go to Shubenacadie Wildlife Park to live out his natural life. Two weeks later, Hope contacted the park to see how the marten was doing. As it happened, Quill managed to escape from there, and no one knows exactly what happened to him, but he probably never survived in the wild due to the issue with his heart. I have a feeling, though, that his little spirit will always be close to Hope, never that far from her, just as he was when he was staying there and recovering at Hope for Wildlife, and I am sure that she will meet him again in the spirit world.

Hope has many stories of wildlife that she has cared for and that have returned to say thank you and good-bye. One such animal was an otter that she cared for and then did a soft release of after a long rehabilitation. Hope was sitting on her balcony sometime later, facing the lake, and suddenly this otter came out of the water and ran up to her and curled up in her lap for a while before it scampered back into the water and was never seen again. She made sure to get lots of pictures to remember that special moment before the otter made its journey back into the wild.

Hope also rehabbed a raccoon once that was missing an ear. It was in the very beginning years of Hope for Wildlife. Once it was all healed, she put it back out into the wild. The following year, some people who live on the island near Hope called her and reported that they had a raccoon living in their attic. They took a video to show her because they thought it was kind of unique looking. Hope saw on the video that the raccoon was nestled there with her babies and that she was missing an ear. It was definitely the raccoon that she had rehabbed, and it was obviously doing well.

She also had a raccoon that came back after it was rehabbed and released out into the wild. He returned all drenched in oil and tar, probably where there had been a lot of road work. He came back looking for help! They got him all cleaned up, of course, but the amazing thing is that this raccoon knew that it could come to Hope for Wildlife for help, even though it was a wild animal and should have been wary of humans.

Another time, a deer, which they had to ear tag when they were rehabbing it, lost its ear tag. They had to tranquilize the deer to give it another one, but this deer happened to wake up quickly from the anesthetic and started to die because it was cold. They had to reverse the anesthetic quickly, and the minute they did that, the deer bolted. Hope still sees her often in the area, and the deer's unique ear tag helps Hope easily identify her as being the deer that had bolted. One year that deer came back to Hope for Wildlife with her baby fawn, and she let Hope get close enough to almost touch her baby. Hope still sees them around at least once or twice a month.

Four or five deer wander up to my house as well, but none of them has an ear tag. They are two females with their young. Hope told me that they see about 50 deer every year, and she and her staff just love seeing them in the wild. They are marvelous creatures.

The deer that visit my yard are quite chunky, so they obviously get a lot of good food to eat, namely my elderberry trees. I also occasionally feed them carrots or apples, but Hope tells me that I shouldn't feed them those sugary foods too often due to their complex digestive system. Giving deer apples and carrots is the equivalent to feeding our children chocolate. Once in a while is all right, but not too often. Deer pellets can be bought at the store and those are good for them and should be included in any mix that might be left out for them. These things are good to know as I like to feed the wildlife that comes to me at my home. Elderberries carry good medicine for us for curing sickness and colds, so maybe the deer just know instinctively that they can have a little bit for their own good. I think they probably know that to some degree.

When we do help wild animals in some way, they do find their way back because they never forget a food source or the kindness and care that they have received. A trust builds up between the animal and the human. Hope has had many animals return to Hope for Wildlife for brief visits and it always brings her joy to know that those animals are still doing well and thriving on their own. As for the raccoons that

Hope rescues, they are now microchipped and are relocated to their own home turf, so that reduces the chances of them returning to look for food.

I told Hope about the fox dens that are along the road that leads to my house and how I often see up to a dozen fox kits or pups out on the road, sleeping and playing with each other like little puppies. It is beautiful to see, but I stop my car and tell them they really should be more careful and not sleep on the pavement!

Out of all the animals that Hope has been able to rehabilitate through her center, the one animal that she has a very strong spiritual connection with is still the marten, and she probably always will. I'm sure that the marten is one of her Animal Totems that she can call upon to lend her its medicine of playful resourcefulness, courage, and determination to survive against all odds. Hope for Wildlife continues to do its good work to help the Animal Nation, and it deserves all the help and support from the public that it can get as a not-for-profit organization.

Some people feel called to be in service to animals. Often people who are drawn to one animal or another, for example, people who have a desire to love and care for horses, dogs, cats, birds, or even fish, probably have a strong totem connection to one of these animals. Some people have a connection to a certain wild or exotic animal, like Hope's connection to the marten. That is one animal that stands out among the many that she has rescued, and it is specific to her. Without having rescued an animal, perhaps we are drawn to a certain type of animal that has a special connection that is very personal to us.

CHAPTER 24

♦ ♦ ♦ ♦

Ekinuwa'taqatite'wk wais+sk aq Ikanintate'ma'timk

ANIMAL MESSENGERS AND FORERUNNERS

We have our own totems that accompany us, but sometimes messages can come to us from the Animal Nation that may guide us through a particular passage in life. Maybe there is a certain time when we need to carry a particular medicine while approaching a situation. The animal may not be our totem, but that doesn't mean that their medicine won't come to us to help us face particular situations or problems that may arise or even just provide us with guidance of some sort. Many times when animals show up in our life, they may not necessarily appear with a profound message, but they could simply be carrying a message from a loved one that says, "Hey, I'm here. I'm with you. I'm around you."

After my father passed, one of the things he used to send me quite often was blue jays. While he was alive, my father played guitar, and so did I. I remember my dad being a very good guitar player, and he liked playing "House of the Rising Sun," but also the Dire Straits song, "Money for Nothing," which I think was one of the last songs he ever played for us. My dad had a pretty good voice, too, and could sing a bit, much better than I can sing. I really appreciated my father's talent.

What I didn't know at the time of his passing was that he had bought me a gift for Christmas before he died, while he was away with the Navy, and it was still on the ship after his passing. When I received my father's gift that Christmas, I thought it was kind of odd that I was getting a gift from him. Then I learned that my dad had already bought it for me a while before he died. It was a guitar with a design of two blue jays on it. Ever since receiving that guitar, blue jays have shown up to remind me that my father is still around me.

Most of the time, if I was struggling in life, I would be surrounded by a bunch of blue jays that would be squawking at me, reminding me that he was there watching over me. There was one day in particular when I was at brunch in Bedford with my mom and we were talking about my father. My mom asked me, "Do you feel like they are still around? I haven't gotten a sign in forever." My stepdad, Larry, had also passed away at this point. When we walked out of the restaurant, lo and behold, right there beside my car door, was a blue jay feather. I picked it up and I said, "Mom, look!" She said, "Oh my God, it's a blue jay feather!" I told her that to answer her question of whether or not they are still around, this was a validation that they were, or at least my dad was still kicking around and reminding us that he was still there. Messages from animals from particular people in the spirit world can show up in our life at any time.

Also, there is a sense of animals giving us a message at a particular time in our life. Maybe we are going through something difficult, and a butterfly comes and lands on us. What does a butterfly represent? Transformation. Another good one is a message that I had gotten from my aunt Nancy after she passed, which was a dragonfly that landed on me. That dragonfly also represents transformation. So, even though the blue jay, the butterfly, and the dragonfly are not my personal totems, they can still carry animal messages to me in my life.

Animal messages can come to us in many different ways. I would say that even if we don't believe that they are our totems, we should be mindful and be open to the messages that all living creatures can bring. There may be a particular medicine that we need at a time in our life about transformation or shift or change, or even just to say, "Hey, I love you and I am with you still. I am still around."

Patricia T., a Spirit Talker Tribe member, wrote to me to relate her experiences of animals as spirit messengers when her son and her mother-in-law both unfortunately died very close to each other, within the same year. The family was understandably very deep in mourning, but Spirit did not forget them and tried to comfort them with their continued presence. Patricia's beloved son Pierre had a tattoo of wolf eyes across his shoulder blades. His last words to his mother before he passed into the spirit world were, "I want you to live a good life and be happy." When the family burned a sacred fire in honor of his grandmother who transitioned the same year as he did, a white wolf came to the sacred fire and looked at the family gathered around. Patricia wrote, "It gave the feels of Spirit."

Then on Thanksgiving, while the entire family was seated eating a meal together, an eagle swooped down to the window and looked inside at everyone. They all "got the feels of Spirit." That same night, Patricia got out of bed, unable to sleep, and sat outside for a bit. A white wolf came out of the tall grass and stayed there watching her. Again, she "got the feels of Spirit."

Patricia's son Palmer is followed by a hawk every time he goes into the bush. Once he asked if it was really his brother sending it to him, and the hawk flew right up to a tree in front of him. He said, "It gave the feels of Spirit." There have been many other signs from Pierre, and one in particular came when the family went to a sweat lodge and the conductor said to them, "Your son has always been with you, and he has shown you in different ways, through a hawk, a wolf, and an eagle. [Your son] says, 'I want you to live a good life and be happy.'" It gave all of them "the feels of Spirit," as the conductor of the sweat ceremony could only have known that if he heard Pierre speaking directly to him in spirit. Patricia knows that her son Pierre is pure infinite light, but a mother's grief is very heavy to carry. These signs from the Animal Nation have helped her and her family as they work through their grief journey.

Another role that animals can sometimes play in our life is as forerunners, announcing things to come. I remember when I was going through some legal issues and I had a bad feeling about them. I was going through a divorce at the time and unfortunately, a blue jay came and hit my front door. The blue jay was stunned. I remember thinking, *I hope this isn't a bad omen.* It turned out that it was a bad omen! I went to court, and things didn't turn out so well. I had to appeal the judgment, and when it did go back to court, it did work out, and things did balance out in my life. It was almost like my dad found a way through a forerunner to warn me of something negative that would happen to give me insight that potentially something was not good. The blue jay didn't die, though. It was just stunned, so I put it in a tree, and it stayed there for a little bit and then flew off. It was something bad, but it turned out to be all right in the end, just like my court case. The blue jay unfortunately hit the door, but it all worked out in time. It seemed like the blue jay was sending me a message from my father giving me a heads-up, saying,

"Maybe things aren't going to go your way today, but everything will work out all right in the end."

Other times there were messages like when my cat Stormy was about to make her journey home to the spirit world and the little bird landed on my car windshield, sending us a message that Spirit was with us at that difficult time. Even though that bird doesn't particularly speak to me in the medicine that I carry in life, it is still a message from the Animal Nation that there are spirits among us. They are very divinely connected to us, and they send us those animals that come to us because they are aware of what we are going through.

Something very cool that happened when I went to visit Hope for Wildlife was that I got to be in an enclosure with a bobcat named Jessie. He came right up to me and was rubbing himself on my legs. Jessie was domesticated and couldn't be released into the wild. I had never met a bobcat in my life before. I got to pet him, rub his head, scratch him behind his ears and his chin, and rub his back; he was actually purring. It was so amazing to have a chance to do that in my lifetime. There must have been a message for me there in the medicine that the bobcat was bringing me, even though I don't feel that it is my totem.

Bobcat Medicine is about balancing alone time with time with others and about trusting our senses and our psychic impressions. It symbolizes independence, clear vision, and self-reliance. Maybe Jessie was trying to teach me that there is true power in silence. If I have been too busy of late, maybe I should take more time to be alone and to contemplate and trust my psychic impressions. It was strange how deeply I connected to the bobcat that day. I feel that he trusted me and showed me unconditional love with his affection. Jessie's inability to care for himself and his total reliance on humans for his care showed up in his affection for me as a human, even though we had never met before.

Even while I was speaking with my ghostwriter, Suzan, about this book, I looked out my window and some deer showed up outside in my yard. I took pictures of them and sent them to her. It made me think of my father, how we never saw even one deer on all the hunting trips we had gone on together. We were never able to get a deer, despite how abundant they are here in Nova Scotia, and suddenly they were showing up right on my front lawn! The timing was perfect, because they showed up just as I was talking about these stories of hunting with my dad. It's amazing that the animals that come to us at different times do so to give us medicine or a message or maybe an insight into something that is coming, or a message that something not so good is about to happen.

As we approach Christmas, I reflect on the story of Elder Danny Paul, when the owl showed up on Christmas Eve. Now one year after the owl first appeared to me, I think about it again. That Owl Medicine came to me showing me how I am to move forward in my next stage in life. It is a totem that I carry, but it also brought a message to let me know that the Elder had made his journey home to the spirit world. Animals will come to us for different reasons, in different ways, with different medicines and messages. Just because we don't think they are our Animal Totems doesn't mean they don't come to us with a message.

Just like the little bird on my windshield was a forerunner letting us know that Stormy was ready to go back to the spirit world, there have been other instances of animals who can forewarn of someone's imminent passing. I remember the story of Oscar the cat who was adopted by a nursing home in Providence, Rhode Island, as a kitten. Oscar would follow the medical staff on their rounds but would not usually stay with any patient for long ... unless that patient was near the end of their life. On those occasions, he would snuggle up and lay with the patients. He predicted this by carefully sniffing the air and then curling up, purring, beside those who were about to make their transition home to the spirit world. I wonder if Spirit had a hand in guiding Oscar's behavior so that patients could feel his comfort at the end of their life. Animals, but cats in particular, are known to be very psychic and have an awareness of journeying home. That little bird could not smell my cat Stormy, who was dying in my arms inside the car, and yet the bird knew and came with a message that Spirit was with us. I think that animals are more aware of spirits than people are sometimes.

Other animals can also be used to sniff things such as disease, like dogs who can sniff out cancer cells in patients. I'll tell the story of a lady who used to be in my online course, Spirit Talker Tribe. Unfortunately, she has since passed away from cancer. Her name was Anamarija Wagner. She told me a story that before she was diagnosed, she had a dog that would come up to her and would keep smelling her breast. He wouldn't leave her breast alone, so it inspired her to go get checked by her doctor and have a breast exam, and sure enough, they found the cancer in her breast that her dog would not stop sniffing. In this case, an animal was using scent, but it came with a message, giving her guidance, a nudge to go to the doctor to discover what she was going through. Her dog must have gotten an intuitive sense from Spirit to alert her that something was not quite right. Animals do have a keen sense of smell, hearing, and sight, but they also are very psychic at different times and are very connected to the spirit world. I think that they sometimes see the spirit world more than most people can.

I feel animals show up in our life at different times, and for some people a certain animal might show up and make them think of a particular loved one, or if an animal shows up in a very strange or unique way, like a bird that hits the window, like it did with me, it could signal something that is about to happen. In Indigenous teachings, we feel that when an owl shows up, there is bad news. In those cases, people don't want to see owls. I don't have that belief, and of course, it's one of my totems, and I think that all animals are amazing. Each carries its own medicine, and I am grateful for whenever they show up and for whatever they are giving me that day. Recently it was a bobcat, and I'm grateful for the encounter that I had with that bobcat. Animals have so much to teach us, and we should be open to receiving their divinely guided messages to us from the spirit world.

CHAPTER 25

♦ ♦ ♦ ♦

Wape'te'w Mestapekiejit
E'pit Ikanaptasikewe'l

WHITE BUFFALO CALF WOMAN AND PROPHECY

Only when the last tree has been cut down and the last fish has been eaten, and the last stream poisoned, will you realize you cannot eat money.

— CREE PROVERB

White Buffalo Calf Woman brought prophecies to the Sioux, Dakota, and Lakota people. She also brought a sacred pipe to the ceremonies. In the end, she turned into a white buffalo calf herself, and the prophecy is that she will return again as a white buffalo. When the white buffalo are born into the world, which I have started to see in more abundance now, I think it is a message about our desperate need to care for Mother Earth. That is where humanity has really gone out of balance. We need to bring balance to the Human Nation as well as the Animal Nation, so that both can live in harmony. There is more construction, urban development, and more devastation to wildlife areas in the world now than ever before.

In Canada, there is still a lot of Crown Land, about 89 percent of the country, actually. It is still kept in its natural state, wild and undeveloped. Thankfully, this land hasn't been bulldozed over and built up with skyscrapers everywhere. Unfortunately, not all countries are like this, and some countries are a lot more out of balance than others.

Many Indigenous communities in Canada that I've been to are doing their part to conserve wildlife, namely the buffalo, as we Indigenous people call it, or bison as it is widely known. When I was out in Sioux Valley, Manitoba, with the Dakota Nation, they had a herd of buffalo that they cared for, and there were many more white buffalo being born. I believe that means that we need to give care back to the Animal Nation, to provide life for them. They have provided life for Indigenous peoples for so long, and now the importance of the prophecy of the White Buffalo Calf Woman is to recognize that the buffalo continues to exist, that we see them, that they have a natural space and place within the world, and that they don't just exist to be hunted. In my opinion, when there is a healthy herd with good numbers, we as Indigenous people can harvest an animal to be used for sustenance and pelts and all other things the animal can give us, without wasting anything. Unless we are doing a sacred ceremony and using them properly, we shouldn't be hunting them at all. They should never be hunted solely for their fur, and their carcasses should not be left to rot in fields. The buffalo are a representation of how humans have overharvested and overdeveloped the land and that we need to think about the preservation of nature and the balance between humans and nature. If we are not careful, one day we will realize that it is too late.

The prophecy of the White Buffalo Calf Woman is so true. Indigenous peoples were out of balance, and she brought her sacred pipe to help us find balance through ceremony. She also symbolizes, through her return to the spirit world as a white buffalo, the need to find balance, because Indigenous people were out of balance with respect to and in connection to ceremonies. She helped bring them back to balance and spiritual harmony. She comes back as a white buffalo within the world that we can see with a message about balance, not just in regard to spirituality and ceremony, but actually about the balance in nature between our modern lifestyle and the natural world that we are surrounded by. We need to preserve and hold sacred the land that the animals live upon because we humans live upon it too. If we fish every fish out of the ocean and poison all the rivers, scrape off all the topsoil from the land, there will be nothing left for us to eat. We won't have fish; we won't have wildlife. We may farm the land, but today's farming is not what it once was.

In California, a Land Back initiative has made it possible for Tom Little Bear Nason, tribal leader of the Esselen Nation, to buy back 14,000 acres of land called Capan. It is situated in the hills of Monterey County. Even though his people were forced from their land, he believes that his people were never really separated from it spiritually, remembering their souls through the trees. Stewardship of the forests is vital to a healthy environment, and along with controlled burning, called cultural fire, and pruning of the oak trees, the people of the Esselen Nation are able to practice once again traditional farming methods that do not strip the land of all its goodness but rather integrate plantings within the existing ecosystem. Native people have tended to forests for thousands of years, caring for sick trees, and because of this practice, they have reduced the risk of devastating wildfires. The US Forestry Service supports this practice as well. Scientists have discovered what the Elders have always believed necessary and have done in the past.

How many of our foods that we are eating have been genetically modified? Even the beef that we eat comes from herds that were fed genetically modified grain. I know Dr. Wayne Dyer had fears of this in the past. He spoke about it publicly. He made an effort to eat as naturally as he possibly could. I subscribe to that philosophy as much as I can as well. How many foods are getting recalled every other day because of contamination? How many of our pets died too young from kidney failure in 2007 because we bought something for them to eat that contained melamine and cyanuric acid? There was a widespread recall of these contaminated foods. Why was melamine in their foods in the first place? There was even concern about these contaminants making their way into the human food supply through its existence in animal feed. If we poison the Animal Nation, we will be in turn poisoning ourselves. This could lead to more disease, more imbalance within us. Our waters have become more toxic as well.

When I went fishing in Newfoundland every summer with my grandfather as I was growing up, there was an abundance of codfish. I have noticed a drop in their numbers over the years because we have overfished them. Recently, when I went back to Newfoundland for a visit, I got a boat. I was really happy to visit my mother's hometown and to spend time out there with different communities that can only be accessed by boat. I did a lot of cod fishing. Sadly, even the cod fishing season there is very limited now because it is only open on a few weekends of the year. It's a food fishery, just for personal consumption. We were only allowed to catch five cod per person and only up to fifteen per day per boat. Between my wife, Michelle, and I both fishing for cod, this was the first time in my 52 years that I found it extremely difficult to catch anything. The water was too warm for cod, so warm that it was difficult to catch my quota of cod for food. I saw how our world is changing so rapidly within my lifetime. I have seen so much change in our environment, in the food that we eat, and this is in just one lifetime.

Everything has been exacerbated by the warming of the planet. It is even worse than we can imagine. Three things that I will never use again in Nova Scotia are cross-country skis, snowshoes, and a snowmobile. We have just recently had the first white Christmas in years. I remember that when I was a child, we used to have such large snowfalls that I could dig snow forts, and I used to go into the woods to check on my rabbit snares with my cross-country skis and my snowshoes, and I even had a snowmobile. Today, all of those things would be useless. If I had skis or even a sled, I would be lucky to use them for maybe a week or two a year. That would be if I were lucky, because whenever it does snow here, it vanishes. It's not like it was when I was a kid, and it would be a waste of money for me to have any of those things, even though I live in Canada! Nova Scotia is warming up faster than any other place in Canada. Even next to us in New Brunswick, they still have an abundance of snow in the winter.

The weather has gotten milder every year in Nova Scotia, and now we are seeing a problem arising in the number of ticks. The deer are infested with ticks carrying Lyme disease, so now I have to check my dogs for ticks after they go outside. We never had this big of a problem with ticks when I was young. Back then, it would get cold enough every winter to kill the ticks. We are not caring enough for our habitat. It's all about oil, gas, money, infrastructures, and making a few people wealthy. That may last a generation or two, but in Indigenous culture, we have a teaching called the Seventh Generation Principle, based on an ancient Haudenosaunee or Iroquois philosophy that says that what we do today should be sustainable and have lasting consequences for the next seven generations. So we should be mindful and think about the impact we will have on the generations that will follow us. I have to make sure that all my descendants have a place in this world and that it will be a place that is sustainable. It is a scary thought that this could potentially be the last seven generations that will be able to survive on the land.

Indigenous people have an approach to caring for the world. There is Western technology that can help us, other than genetically modifying our food. Indigenous people wish to bring both world views together to achieve balance. The Indigenous Mi'kmaq people call it Etuaptmumk, which is a Mi'kmaq word for "Two-Eyed Seeing," which seeks to integrate Indigenous and Western knowledge systems to benefit all. This term was first coined by Mi'kmaq Elders Albert and Murdena Marshall of Eskasoni First Nation, and it is about viewing Indigenous wisdom with one eye and Western knowledge with the other and making the two eyes work together in harmony to better our planet. Its main principles are based on finding harmony between two viewpoints to achieve balance, sustainability, and accountability.

I think if there is anything I can leave behind in regard to the White Buffalo Calf Woman prophecy and about the white buffalo coming back into the world, it would be that we have to work together. Indigenous people lend the world the wisdom that we have about the environment and that balance of not overfishing, overhunting, or taking more than we need, sustaining the environment in which we live. When I am picking sweet grass or berries, I make sure that I leave some. I don't pick all the fiddleheads either, and I make sure that I take them off only at the head and not at the roots, so that there will be some for the next year to grow back. I am always thinking about the future, because if I just take them all, there won't be any in the future.

With Etuaptmumk, which is Two-Eyed Seeing, we can achieve a balance in the world to protect first and foremost the Animal Nation, the harmony and balance of nature. We must protect our Earth; if not, our seventh great-grandchildren won't have a place in this world. We won't be able to sustain life on this planet for very much longer if we keep going the way we are, so we need to find a way to come together and think about how to make this work in a good way. We see the technology that Western civilization has, and we apply it to Indigenous understanding.

The Sioux Valley First Nation and their herd of buffalo, as well as other First Nations people, are caring for the buffalo and raising their numbers enough so that they can gradually be released back into the wild and be brought back from near extinction numbers, to give them an opportunity to flourish again. The people of the Okanagan Nation in British Columbia, who are part of the salmon industry where they are raising salmon and releasing them back into the wild, are also a good example of stewardship of the Animal Nation.

I think that there is wisdom that both cultures, Western and Indigenous, have to share, and we need to work together to create a more sustainable and healthier world for the Animal Nation and for ourselves so that the next seven generations of people that follow us will have a place within this world. This is the true embodiment of the Beaver Wisdom, one of the Seven Grandfather Teachings. Whatever we do to the world will be felt for the next seven generations.

We can already see the coming together of these two cultures when Indigenous people rely on Western medicine to vaccinate and deworm the herds of buffalo, keeping them safe in enclosed areas much like cattle, until they are healthy enough in number to be set free. Indigenous philosophy regarding the buffalo is already there. Some buffalo may also occasionally be harvested within a community, as it is their culture to share a meal in the traditional way and to use all parts of the buffalo to make drums, rattles, and any other ceremonial objects as our ancestors have done before. Of course this is done with the highest respect for the buffalo, with ceremony and medicine offered to give thanks for the animal's life. The integration of Western culture in the preservation of the environment should be for the betterment of the Animal Nation, and we can see the interconnectedness of Etuaptmumk especially within the Buffalo Nation. Integrating Indigenous wisdom with Western technology can save our world, creating a sustainable environment to support all Nations that live upon Mother Earth. We must ask ourselves what we can do to be of service in leaving the world in a better way for the next seven generations.

Prayer to White Buffalo Calf Woman

Sacred White Buffalo Calf Woman,
Bearer of wisdom, balance, and harmony,
I call upon your gentle spirit
To guide my heart and hands in caring for Mother Earth.

You, who brought the sacred pipe,
And taught the ways of living in harmony,
Show me how to walk gently upon this land,
With gratitude for all that it provides.

Teach me to see the Earth as sacred,
Each grain of soil, each drop of water,
As gifts of life, deserving of reverence and care.
May I honor the animals, plants, and stones
As my kin in this shared journey of existence.

Help me find compassion within myself,
To take only what I need and to give back in return.
Grant me the wisdom to use resources wisely
And the courage to protect what is fragile and irreplaceable.

May I nurture the land as a mother nurtures her child,
With patience, love, and devotion.
May my actions honor your teachings
And ensure that the next seven generations inherit a world
As beautiful and abundant as the one we've been given.

White Buffalo Calf Woman,
Walk beside me, so that I may learn Two-Eyed Seeing,

To blend Indigenous wisdom with Western ways
And to live as a caretaker of Mother Earth.

I honor you, your spirit and teachings.

Msit No'kmaq—All my relations.

◆ ◆ ◆ ◆

CHAPTER 26

◆ ◆ ◆ ◆

Pemaptutioq Ki'lew aq To'tmuaq

WALKING WITH YOUR TOTEMS

As an Indigenous person, I think it's important to share my personal journey through life and my connection to culture by helping others understand their journey, because we each have an individual journey, and no two people are exactly alike. People don't have to be Indigenous to be connected to the Animal Nation. There are so many Indigenous cultures from around the world, like the Sámi people of Northern Europe and the Aboriginal people of Australia, as well as all peoples from South America to North America and other places. It is important to note that the Animal Nation is celebrated by all peoples from all countries all around the world and is not solely a North American Indigenous tradition.

I think we have forgotten our spiritual connection to the Animal Nation within our life and how animals may guide us spiritually, mentally, and physically with their sacred power. The Animal Nation possesses sacred power that can protect us. When these things are more fully known to us, then we can engage with the spirit world in a much greater and more profound way.

If I were to draw comparisons between different philosophies and religions of pre-Christian times, there was a deeper connection, more so than can be found in today's common knowledge of spirituality, about the Animal Nation. It was when Christianity came to Turtle Island that these beliefs were subverted and were redirected toward more Angelic beings, although they are humanoid beings with animalistic qualities, namely possessing wings like birds. Some Spirit Animals are even attributed to these Angelic beings. I do not wish to take anything away from Angelic beings, because I feel they exist and they have a place within the spirit world itself as well.

Regardless, I think that it is time that we remember the Animal Nation and our cross-cultural dependence on animals, not only for food but also for companionship, love, and kindness, for the tools that Indigenous people make from them and all the resources of life that we would use them for. We also have a deep spiritual connection with them. We should honor them, much like in the old belief systems of the Celts and the Egyptians, who would have carried representations of these animals as sacred objects. I have many sacred objects connected to the Animal Nation, from eagle feathers to polar bear claws, polar bear rugs and owl feathers. They have all come to me at specific times in my life.

My hope is that people who have read this book will not only benefit from my journey but that they will also discover their own personal journey with their Spirit Totem Animals. What I've realized is that there are four stages of life that I've been taught through the Medicine Wheel teachings, and that it is through these stages of life that different animals have come to me for different reasons, whether it be as Spirit Totems or Power Totems. They are all deeply connected to me, and I carry their medicines with me through life. I celebrate their energy, their medicine, and I incorporate them in my life as greatly as I can. I hope that when people have read this book, read my stories, and have learned more about Spirit Totem Animals, they too will have a deeper and stronger connection to their own Spirit Totem and Power Totem Animals, as well as the Animal Nation as a whole, and incorporate them into their lives.

Our purpose is to find our own connections, incorporating ancient wisdom about the Animal Nation as part of the spirit team that watches over us and walks beside us in life, imparting their strengths and their wisdom to aid us along our journey. We are all one, and our spirits blend together in unison with the Animal Nation and also with the whole natural world, as is the Indigenous tradition and belief system.

We have a responsibility to keep each other well through caring for the environment, through the food and resources that we use and rely on each other for. Without one or the other, we could not survive. The Human Nation and the Animal Nation live in balance and harmony with one another, and we must help them in different ways. Humans have also hurt the Animal Nation; therefore, it is our duty to do our best to restore balance and harmony between the natural world and our human existence, which is largely dependent upon technology in our modern times. When that balance was lost, some animals went extinct.

There are a lot of animals that exist in the spirit world that no longer exist in physical form anymore because they have gone extinct, unfortunately because of humanity. There are many that are still here, though, that we can still have a deep spiritual connection to and that are still thriving within the world and that may need our help and support. What they give us, spiritually and physically, we have to give back to them. When we think of Spirit Totem Animals, that involves the human physical nation and the animal physical nation that exists upon the world, helping and serving each other in a reciprocal relationship. This may be a spiritually based book, but we also have to keep in mind that we have a role to play in balancing the world so that we can all have life and continue this existence upon Mother Earth, and hopefully live together harmoniously.

We need to cherish animals that are in the physical world and realize the importance that they have to us in the spiritual realm as well. Today, we do celebrate animals in a particular way, because we have brought them in as pets. They are part of our families, and we have incorporated them into our family connections, but it doesn't end with cats, dogs, budgies, and goldfish. There are a lot of other animals in the world that are still deeply connected to us too. Not only do they rely on us, but we also rely on them for sustenance, whether it is cattle, chickens, fish, elk, moose, or deer that we harvest to supply for us.

We know that we have a spiritual connection, but we have a physical connection as well. We have to honor both of those connections within life in a good way. Expressing gratitude for everything that comes to us for our sustenance is one way of honoring the Animal Nation. We have to be grateful for the life that animals give up for us and the life that they give to us. There is also an energy that animals give to us that transcends just food, a spiritual connection, and in some cases there may even be a pet connection.

All animals are unique and special in their own way, and they all have different medicines that they can share. I feel that some of us carry particular medicines, and we may be drawn to particular animals. Whatever that is for the individual and at whatever stage in life that they come to us, I think that by having read this book and by doing the exercises within it, we can discover our uniquely different Animal Totems, whether within Infancy, Youth, Adulthood, or the Elder phase of life. We will realize that there are certain animals that we connect to more strongly. We will feel more drawn to them, and they may provide messages of light, help, and guidance that we didn't really recognize before, and that we will see to a greater extent. Hopefully we will become better stewards of the Animal Nation so that together, with all of humanity, we can live upon this world in a good way, in balance and harmony.

Now that we are at the end of this book and you have read many of my stories, and you have done the exercises to discover your own Power and Spirit Totem Animals, it is important that you work with their medicines. I challenge you to speak to them, saying specific heartfelt prayers to your totems that call upon their medicines to be utilized in your life. Honor them in your daily spiritual practice and personal ceremonies, and invite them to guide you through life in a good way.

Wela'lin, Msit No'kmaq.
Thank you, all my relations.

ACKNOWLEDGMENTS

♦ ♦ ♦ ♦

This book would not have been possible without the dedicated effort of many people, but most especially my ghostwriter Suzan Bizier for helping me put my stories and ideas into the written word.

Thanks go out to Hay House author Asha Frost for writing the foreword, and to Anne Marie Marchand for providing Mi'kmaq translations.

I would like to thank all the contributing Spirit Talker Tribe members for sharing with me their stories of how the Animal Nation has helped them in their life journey. I hope that they will continue to share their stories to heal the hearts of many.

To the many Elders that have come to me in my life all across Canada who have shared with me their wisdom and their teachings about Indigenous culture and the Animal Nation, I say Wela'lioq, thank you all.

To the generous people who have gifted me Animal Medicine that I work with every day as a spirit talker, I offer my deepest gratitude. Thank you Andre Chevalier; Elder Joe; Barbara Kent Bishop; Kelly Finnegan and her husband, Steve Dunbrack; Linda Harris; John Mormile; and others.

I would also like to thank my two daughters, Mackenzie and Sianna, for our shared love of our cat Stormy and for all the Animal Nation. You make me immensely proud.

I am forever grateful to the ones I love in the spirit world who have consistently communicated their love and guidance to me through the Animal Nation: to Larry for sending me the eagle, to my father for sending me blue jays and the moose and the deer, to my aunt Nancy for sending me the dragonfly, and to Elder Danny Paul for sending me the snowy owl, I give you my thanks. I acknowledge your messages to me.

I, of course, would like to thank the team at Hay House, my literary agent, Michele Martin and my editor, Anna Cooperberg, who make all of this possible.

Lastly, I want to thank my lovely and devoted wife, Michelle Beaupre, for supporting me as my partner in life.

Wela'lioq, thank you all.

ABOUT THE AUTHOR

♦ ♦ ♦ ♦

SHAWN LEONARD is a heart-centered Mi'kmaq psychic medium and the star and host of the APTN TV show *Spirit Talker.* He is also the author of the national bestseller *Spirit Talker* and *Wisdom of the Elders Oracle.* His authentic approach to his readings, live shows, and media appearances has changed the hearts and minds of many, bringing healing and hope to those who have loved ones in the spirit world. He teaches spirit communication and imparts his wisdom and knowledge of the spirit world in his Spirit Talker Tribe online course to hundreds of students each year. He has appeared on the Next Level Soul podcast with Alex Ferrari, and his show, *Spirit Talker,* is available on Next Level Soul TV to audiences globally. If you would like to learn more about Shawn and his work, you can find him at **SHAWN-LEONARD.COM.**

Hay House Titles of Related Interest

YOU CAN HEAL YOUR LIFE, the movie,
starring Louise Hay & Friends
(available as an online streaming video)
www.hayhouse.co.uk/louise-movie

THE SHIFT, the movie,
starring Dr Wayne W. Dyer
(available as an online streaming video)
www.hayhouse.co.uk/the-shift-movie

♦ ♦ ♦

THE ANIMAL ELDERS ORACLE: A 44-Card Deck & Guidebook of Indigenous Wisdom & Healing Medicine, by Asha Frost

YOU ARE THE MEDICINE: 13 Moons of Indigenous Wisdom, Ancestral Connection and Animal Spirit Guidance, by Asha Frost

INTUITIVE ANIMAL COMMUNICATION: Co-Create a Meaningful Life and Deep Connection with Animals, by Michael Burke

WOMAN BETWEEN THE WORLDS: A Call to Your Ancestral and Indigenous Wisdom, by Apela Colorado, PhD

All of the above are available at your local bookstore,
or may be ordered by contacting Hay House (see next page).

♦ ♦ ♦

We hope you enjoyed this Hay House book. If you'd like to receive our online catalogue featuring additional information on Hay House books and products, please contact:

Hay House UK Ltd
1st Floor, Crawford Corner,
91–93 Baker Street, London W1U 6QQ
Tel: +44 (0)20 3927 7290; www.hayhouse.co.uk

Published in the United States of America by:
Hay House LLC
PO Box 5100, Carlsbad, CA 92018-5100
Tel: (760) 431-7695 or (800) 654-5126
www.hayhouse.com

Published in Australia by:
Hay House Australia Publishing Pty Ltd
18/36 Ralph St., Alexandria NSW 2015
Tel: +61 (02) 9669 4299
www.hayhouse.com.au

Published in India by:
Hay House Publishers (India) Pvt Ltd
Muskaan Complex, Plot No. 3,
B-2, Vasant Kunj, New Delhi 110 070
Tel: +91 11 41761620
www.hayhouse.co.in

Let Your Soul Grow

Experience life-changing transformation – one video at a time – with guidance from the world's leading experts.

www.healyourlifeplus.com

TRANSFORM YOUR DAY—ANYTIME, ANYWHERE

With the **Empower You** Unlimited Audio *App*

> ⭐⭐⭐⭐⭐ **Life changing.**
> My fav app on my entire phone, hands down! – Gigi

Unlimited access to the entire Hay House audio library!

You'll get:

- 600+ soul-stirring **audiobooks** to expand your mind
- 1,000+ **meditations** for restful sleep, morning focus, and gentle healing
- Bite-sized audios **under 20 minutes**—perfect for busy days
- **Exclusive talks** you won't find anywhere else
- **Daily affirmations**
- Fresh content added **every week** to fuel your journey

Listen to the audio version of this book!

> Driving, yard work, and housework have been **transformed**!
> – Ruffles27

Scan the QR code to start listening or visit **hayhouse.com/unlimited**

HAY HOUSE
Online Video Courses

Your journey to a better life starts with figuring out which path is best for you. Hay House Online Courses provide guidance in mental and physical health, personal finance, telling your unique story, and so much more!

LEARN HOW TO:

- choose your words and actions wisely so you can tap into life's magic
- clear the energy in yourself and your environments for improved clarity, peace, and joy
- forgive, visualize, and trust in order to create a life of authenticity and abundance
- manifest lifelong health by improving nutrition, reducing stress, improving sleep, and more
- create your own unique angelic communication toolkit to help you to receive clear messages for yourself and others
- use the creative power of the quantum realm to create health and well-being

To find the guide for your journey, visit www.HayHouseU.com.

HAY HOUSE
online learning

CONNECT WITH
HAY HOUSE
ONLINE

🌐 hayhouse.co.uk   **f** @hayhouse

📷 @hayhouseuk   🦋 @hayhouseuk.bsky.social

♪ @hayhouseuk   ▶ @HayHousePresents

Find out all about our latest books & card decks • Be the first to know about exclusive discounts • Interact with our authors in live broadcasts • Celebrate the cycle of the seasons with us • Watch free videos from your favourite authors • Connect with like-minded souls

'The gateways to wisdom and knowledge are always open.'

Louise Hay